An Analytical Study Of Counseling Theory And Practice With Recommendations For The Philosophy Of Counseling

This dissertation was conducted under the direction of the Reverend Michael J. McKeough, O.Praem, Ph.D., as major professor, and was approved by Miss Marie Corrigan, M.A., and the Reverend Robert P. Mohan, S.S., Ph.D., as Readers.

THE CATHOLIC UNIVERSITY OF AMERICA

An Analytical Study Of Counseling Theory And Practice With Recommendations For The Philosophy Of Counseling

A DISSERTATION
SUBMITTED TO THE FACULTY OF THE GRADUATE SCHOOL OF ARTS
AND SCIENCES OF THE CATHOLIC UNIVERSITY OF AMERICA
IN PARTIAL FULFILLMENT OF THE REQUIREMENTS
FOR THE DEGREE OF DOCTOR OF PHILOSOPHY

by

DOMINIC BRADY, O.P.

The Catholic University of America Press
Washington, D. C.
1952

PROVIDENCE
COLLEGE
LIBRARY

Revisores Ordinis:

        Jacobus McDonald, O. P., S.T.D.
        Sylvester Considine, O.P., S.T.M.

Imprimi potest:

        Eduardus Hughes, O.P., S.T.Lr.
                            Prior Provincialis

Nihil obstat:

        Jacobus McDonald, O.P., S.T.D.
                                Censor Librorum

Imprimatur:

        ✠Henricus P. Rohlman, D.D.
                          Archiepiscopus Dubuquiensis

Die 17 Juli 1952

Copyright, 1952
The Catholic University of America Press, Inc.

Printed by
The Telegraph Herald
Dubuque, Iowa

To Father Walter Farrell, and the Dominican traditions that nurtured his wisdom and fostered his magnanimity.

PREFACE

Contemporary interest in the theory and practice of counseling, and the common acceptance of counseling's valuable service to man in his approach to human maturity are well authenticated facts of our everyday experience. These facts very probably constitute a clear and definitive testament to the inadequacies and limitations of man's creatural potentialities, as well as to his essentially social nature, with its correlative of dependence. Men need other men to help them to know and grow in the perfection of truth and being to which our nature and its Author incline us, but which each individual must grasp alone.

Convictions such as these, added to the evidence of controversy about counseling theory and practice, confidence in the solidity and relevance of Thomistic philosophical principles, and the comprehension of the relationship of limited but perfectible human powers to the natural maturity and happiness that all men so ardently desire, have all urged the undertaking of this study.

The results have been both significant and gratifying. These results have increased the writer's appreciation of the contribution that counseling can make to the perfection of human nature, and have generated a trust that they will be helpful to others for the same purpose. The principles of St. Thomas Aquinas have been of inestimable value in the clarification of the nature and goal of the counseling process, and they function as the reasonable measure of the methods to be selected for its successful completion.

If the results of this study seem meager to some, it is hoped that the insufficiencies will be attributed to the limitation of proceeding in the order of nature alone, and to the intrinsic complexities of the problems that lie at the very center of these matters. Much work remains to be done. Many paths have been opened up to future research and clarification. There is a particular need for experimental evidence to validate and amplify the effectiveness of counseling methodology that it may accomplish the purposes to which it is naturally ordered.

The writer takes this occasion to thank his former Provincial, the Very Reverend Peter O'Brien, O.P., S.T.M., for the opportunity to pursue graduate studies, and his present Provincial, the Very Reverend Edward L. Hughes, O.P., S.T.Lr., for his considerate interest in the completion of this work. A debt of deep gratitude is acknowledged to the Reverend Michael J. McKeough, O.Praem., Ph.D. and Miss Marie Corrigan, M.A., of the Catholic University for their patient concern and kindly direction throughout the writing of this dissertation. Grateful acknowledgment is also due to the Reverend Robert P. Mohan, S.S., Ph.D., for reading the manuscript and his helpful suggestions. Sincere appreciation must be expressed for the charitable and constant encouragement that has been received by the writer from all his Dominican brothers, and especially from the late Very Reverend Walter Farrell, O.P., S.T.M., the Very Reverend Sebastian E. Carlson, O.P., S.T.D., S.T.M., the Very Reverend James J. McDonald, O.P., S.T.D., B.S.T., Reverend Thomas U. Mullaney, O.P., S.T.D., and the Reverend Thomas C. Donlan, O.P., S.T.D. For the preparation of the manuscript, sincere thanks are due to Miss Gertrude M. Phillips, T.O.P.

Grateful acknowledgment is also made to the following publishers for permission to quote material copywrited in their name: Benziger Brothers, Harper and Brothers, Houghton Mifflin Company, McGraw-Hill Book Company, The National Society for the Study of Education, and Sheed and Ward.

TABLE OF CONTENTS

Chapter	Page
I. THE STATEMENT OF THE PROBLEM	1

    The Existence of the Problem
    Fundamental Distinctions Limiting Problem
        Personnel Work
        Guidance
        Counseling
    Sources of Investigation

II. CURRENT SCHOOLS OF COUNSELING ... 17

    The Traditional School
        Arthur Jones
        Ruth Strang
        Edmund G. Williamson
        Robert H. Mathewson
    The Non-Directive School
        Carl R. Rogers

III. COMPARISON AND IMPLICATIONS OF CURRENT THEORIES ... 51

    Agreements and Differences
        General Points of Agreement
        Differences in Regard to the Nature of Counseling
        Differences in Regard to the Aims of Counseling
        Differences in Methods
    Philosophical and Psychological Implications

IV. THE PHILOSOPHICAL SETTING FOR COUNSELING ... 69

    Human Actions and Self-Mastery
    Virtue and Human Self-Mastery
    The Virtue of Prudence and Self-Mastery
        The Meaning of Prudence
        The Nature of Prudence
        Prudence and the Moral Virtues
        The Acts of Prudence
            Counsel
            Judgment
            Command as the Perfection of Prudence
        The Integral Parts of Prudence

V. THE PSYCHOLOGICAL SETTING FOR
COUNSELING 89
 The Acquisition of Prudence and Moral Virtue
  The Acquisition of Virtue in General
  The Acquisition of Total Prudence
 Interaction of Intellect and Will in
 Prudential Operation
  Order of Desire
  Order of Choice
  Order of Execution
 Functional Aspects of Prudential Acts and
 the Integral Parts
  Counsel and Judgment
   Reason
   Memory
   Understanding
   Docility
   Sagacity
  Command of Action
   Foresight
   Circumspection
   Caution

VI. PRUDENCE THROUGH COUNSELING 109
 Prudential Framework for Counseling
 Prudence and the Counseling Process
 Prudence and Counseling Methods
 Counseling Theory and Practice Evaluated
  The Nature of Counseling
  The Aims of Counseling
  The Methods of Counseling

BIBLIOGRAPHY 122

CHAPTER I

THE STATEMENT OF THE PROBLEM

The Existence of the Problem

Little more than a passing acquaintance with the contemporary demands of the reading public for psychological literature is needed to indicate the necessity for this type of information. It seems that the average American, for the moment at least, has lost some of the confidence which has long been attributed to him as a property of his personality. Whatever the cause may be it is clear that tensions, doubts, fears, and indecision are generally recognized as important factors in everyday life.

The vast amount of literature concerned with the problems of guidance, psychotherapy, and counseling, the number of courses preparing for activity in this field, and the selection and training of counselors for high schools, colleges, industry, and the institutions of all sorts is, no doubt, a response to a real need. Textbooks, the plethora of articles and journals that are specially devoted to these questions are all indicative of an active interest in every type of counseling. The real or apparent need for counseling services is again indicated by the large number who seek help at the various agencies specifically established for this purpose.

The assumption that counseling has become a very important field and one that should be worthy of fruitful investigation is not without foundation. That it does deserve careful consideration may be gathered from the fact that counseling, expressly recognized as such or implicitly practiced, is a part of many of our institutions. Student-counseling has for some time been recognized, theoretically at least, as an essential part of good educational procedure. Social and professional work of all types must often begin and sometimes end with a counseling situation.

Thus aside from the popular demand for counseling services there is reason for a great deal of intelligent study in this field of human relationship.

This latter fact is soon realized by anyone who makes a sincere attempt to keep abreast of the current publications. Such a student cannot help noticing that unanimity is not a marked characteristic of all the work that is being done in this field. Intensive study of the textbooks and periodical literature dealing with personnel work, guidance, and counseling is apt to leave the student somewhat confused. That this confusion is not entirely due to the student's lack of comprehensive ability is more than a suspicion. The editor of the *Harvard Educational Review* offered these corroborative words as the preface to an illuminating article on counseling:

> As popular interest in educational, vocational, psychological and other types of counseling has grown, theory and practice in these fields have become increasingly diversified, thus making a unified understanding of the counseling process virtually impossible for the non-specialist, and difficult even for the specialist.[1]

While it is consoling to the confused student to find that others are aware of the difficulties involved in any attempt to arrive at a unified "understanding of the counseling process," this consolation does little toward a solution of these difficulties. Much more than this is required. The zealous student, cognizant of the factors involved, finds in this confusion a challenge to further study. Research and reflection soon lead him to the conviction that has been well expressed by Mathewson.

> Practical problems which confront us in the field of professional personnel work require solution in terms of professional principles based upon a view of counseling as a distinct, definable process.[2]

While such a reasonable position is not without precedent in counseling literature, it is a reflection of a rather recent trend in this field, a trend that is encouraging to those who have been taught to distinguish carefully between the levels of principle,

---

[1] *Harvard Educational Review*, XVII (Winter, 1947), 10.

[2] Robert Mathewson, *Guidance Policy and Practice* (New York: Harper and Brothers, 1949), p. 193.

policy, and practice. It is generally accepted that from the point of view of thinking, the level of principle, which is universal in nature, should always be considered first, with the levels of policy and practice coming second and third. Until principles are established, policy cannot be expressed by general rules, nor can particular decisions be intelligently made in the light of general policy.

For these reasons many of the practical problems of personnel work, such as whether one type of counseling activity or another will be advocated, whether one type of professional training or another shall be followed, whether one organizational procedure or another is to be used, can be brought to an intelligent solution only in the light of the principles which govern the process of counseling.

This commendable trend toward definition, clarification of concepts, and the enunciation of principles may very well be one of the good results of a controversy which has arisen among professional counselors. The occasion of this conflict was the publication, in 1942, of *Counseling and Psychotherapy: Newer Concepts in Practice* by Carl Rogers, Ph.D., then of Ohio State University and now a professor of psychology at the University of Chicago.[3] This book and the subsequent work of both Rogers and his students have been the source of much discussion, and in some quarters, of violent reactions. That these developments were not entirely beyond the expectations of Rogers may be gathered from his words recorded in the preface of his book:

> This book, . . . attempts to state the author's conviction that counseling may be a knowable, predictable, understandable process, a process which can be learned, tested, refined and improved. It is presented with the hope that it will lead counselors and therapists, both in the field and in training, to undertake further investigations, in theory and practice, which will enable us to deepen and perfect our knowledge of ways of enabling the individual to develop a more satisfying adjustment.[4]

It seems safe to say that no single bit of work in the field of counseling has done more to upset the "adjustment" of pro-

[3] Carl R. Rogers, *Counseling and Psychotherapy* (New York: Houghton Mifflin Co., 1942), p. 450.

[4] *Ibid.*, p. ix.

fessional counselors than the publication of Rogers' book. The presentation of his newer concepts in counseling has proved to be a real challenge to traditional thought in regard to the theory and practice of counseling. A great deal of rethinking of the older and more widely accepted ideas has been undertaken. With this rethinking have come greater precision and clarity in the expression of these ideas. More interest has been manifested in determining the nature of the counseling process in itself and as it affects the activity of the counselor and the activity of the client, than was previously in evidence. Emphasis has noticeably shifted from a preoccupation with diagnosis and instruments of appraisal to a more exacting analysis of the counseling interview described by Rogers as the "face-to-face situation through which an effort to alter attitudes, choices, and behavior is made."

While many of the more recent publications in this field indicate decided efforts toward raproachment between the older and newer concepts of counseling it appears that much more remains to be done. This view follows from the consideration of a conviction that has been clearly expressed by Rogers himself:

It is difficult to exaggerate the differences in viewpoint between traditional counseling, as reported by Darley, and the client-centered or non-directive approach advocated by Rogers and Allen. Research must provide the final answer, perhaps in some as yet unformulated frame of reference. Meanwhile, the differences will undoubtedly promote constructive efforts to study this whole field.[5]

Because of these facts and with this attitude in mind an analytical study of current theory and practice in counseling has been undertaken. Through this study it is hoped that the extent of these differences can be determined as well as their implications from the point of view of scholastic thought. This latter task is a necessary part of the problem, particularly, although by no means exclusively, because this study is undertaken in the interest of the Catholic counselor who may be reasonably expected to have a preference for the scholastic frame of reference.

[5] Carl R. Rogers, "Counseling," *Review of Educational Research*, XV (1945), 156-59.

THE STATEMENT OF THE PROBLEM

It is hoped, also, that the non-Catholic counselors will be catholic enough in their outlook so that they too may profit by this study. That this hope is not unfounded follows from the conviction that the scholastic system provides a total view of reality which is more in conformity with demonstrated facts than any other conceptual scheme. Rudolf Allers, a professor at Georgetown University, a man of broad knowledge and vast experience in the fields of philosophy, medicine, and applied psychology, has made this illuminating observation regarding this point:

> In truth, if the principles of Thomistic anthropology were applied to the practical problems of psychology as they become apparent in counseling or in psychotherapy they would prove a great help and contribute in a noteworthy manner towards the clarification of many still very obscure questions. The counselor desirous of basing his work on the solid foundations of a reliable philosophy cannot do better than bring together these two: his knowledge of Thomistic principles, and the empirical facts gathered by the untiring efforts of psychologists, psychiatrists, and physicians.[6]

The Formulation of the Problem

In the light of the foregoing discussion it seems clear that there are three aspects of the problem which present themselves for extensive investigation. While each of these aspects might be worthy of a more lengthy treatment at another time it is believed that they can be presented profitably in one study. The first of these is concerned with the analysis of the nature, aims, and methods of counseling as they are proposed by leading authorities in the field to determine differences and agreements as well as the philosophical implications of their theories; the second, is the establishment of a philosophical and psychological setting for the theory and practice of counseling according to scholastic authorities. The third involves the critical evaluation of current theory and practice of counseling in view of the scholastic framework.

---

[6] Rudolf Allers, "Guidance and Counseling," *American Ecclesiastical Review*, CXIII (1945), 125.

The first task is to analyze the writings of representative authorities in the field of guidance and counseling to determine their exact views on the nature and aims of counseling. Having accomplished this, in the light of the distinction previously mentioned between principle, policy, and practice, one may logically consider their proposed counseling methods. Methods of counseling should flow from the principles which regulate the understanding of both the nature of counseling in itself and the goals to which the process is ordered. It may be mentioned in passing, that because of the practical nature of counseling the goal of the process itself stands as a principle which has a necessary connection with the right understanding of that process. The second chapter of this study in which the analysis will be undertaken, will be divided into two major parts: the first place will be given to the study of the nature, aims, and methods of counseling proposed by representatives of the traditional school; in the second place the same analysis will be made of the concepts proposed by Rogers and his followers, whom it seems reasonable to group under the heading of the New or Client-Centered School of counseling.

The first half of the third chapter will be devoted to a comparative study of the concepts which have been crystallized in the previous chapter. An attempt will be made to isolate whatever differences and agreements there may or may not be between the two schools of thought. As pointed out, it is Rogers' opinion that there is a notable difference in viewpoint between his theory of counseling and that whcih has been more generally held by traditional counselors. The latter, however, do not all agree with Rogers regarding the extent of these differences. Indeed, some seem unwilling to admit that there are any major differences at all. Through careful consideration in this study it is expected that an objective evaluation of these claims can be made.

The second half of the third chapter will be devoted to the philosophical and psychological implications of these theories of counseling. This latter task will be of particular significance to the Catholic counselor. When it is realized that counseling is a process intimately concerned with human acts, which is just another way of saying moral acts, it becomes immediately evident that the process involves much more than psychology is competent to deal with. An appreciation of moral science would seem most necessary for any real competency in this field. Similarly, it is to be expected that, in varying degrees, the moral views of the counselors will be reflected in their theory of the counseling process. It is the intention of this study to uncover these views as they affect the counseling process, and to show their significance in relation to the scholastic synthesis both from the point of view of moral philosophy and moral psychology.

Having demonstrated, in general, the relationship of counseling and the counseling process to scholastic principles of moral science one may reasonably consider whatever that science has to offer for the true appreciation of the problems of counseling. This will be attempted in the fourth and fifth chapters of this study.

The first investigation will be directed to the philosophical setting for counseling. Preliminary investigation indicates that this can be found in the treatment of the virtue of prudence, the habit of reasonable self-rule.

The psychological setting for counseling will be the subject of investigation and demonstration in the fifth chapter. At the completion of this chapter it is hoped that all the material needed to establish an overall framework for the scholastic evaluation and implementation of the theory and practice of counseling will be at hand. The sixth and last chapter will be devoted to a summary and to any significant conclusions that may be arrived at concerning the field of counseling.

With these introductory remarks and without further elucidation, the extent of the investigation undertaken in this study may be succinctly stated as follows: This is a rational analysis and evaluation of the nature, aims, and methods of counseling proposed by current schools with recommendations for the theory and practice of counseling.

Fundamental Distinctions Limiting Problem

It seems advisable to make certain distinctions in regard to the terminology which has been used in the above discussion. These distinctions are necessary for clarity and for the purpose of limiting the topic of investigation within reasonable bounds.

Although these distinctions have already been implied they will be made explicit to obviate misunderstanding.

Counseling is practiced in many institutions other than schools and colleges. It is neither a newly discovered process of this age, nor is it peculiar to the field of education. It is, perhaps, as old as man and may represent a fundamental need of his nature. This study is specifically interested in counseling as good educational procedure and as a function of the formal educational process. Even though this aspect of counseling cannot be completely separated from the more universal applications of the process, it appears wiser to study counseling under these limitations. The principal concern will be the nature, aims, and methods of counseling as they affect and are effective instruments in formal educational agencies, in schools and colleges.

Immediately after having made the above precision, one sees the need for more precise distinctions. In educational literature the terms "counseling" and "guidance" are often used interchangeably. The understanding of their exact signification is further complicated by the frequent interjection of the terms "personnel work" in any discussion of them. Whether this is justifiable or not is not to be determined at this point, nor is a lengthy consideration of the exact formalities in order. For the practical purposes of this study it seems sufficient to make clear an accepted understanding of these terms, and to indicate their relationship to the subject of this study.

By the term *personnel work* is understood all those activities carried on within the school which have as their purpose the adaptation of the school facilities to the peculiar and distinctive needs of individual students. It has probably risen to significance in educational parlance as a response to the doctrine of individual differences, with which educationists have become increasingly impressed with each advance of the measurement movement. It is a generic term resulting from an educational point of view which emphasizes the individual and his all-around development,[7] in order that his total edu-

[7] William H. Cawley, "The Nature of Personnel Work," *Educational Record*, XVIII (1936), 198-266.

cational experience may be most effectively related to his personal needs and potentialities.[8]

Germane and Germane have made this summation of the personnel point of view as it affects the attitude of the educationists:

> When one's philosophy of education is deeply tinged with the personnel point of view, he thinks of the whole school plant . . . as having one purpose, that is, to help each individual to discover his potentialities as to make the most of his life both in and out of school. He believes that the school's main function is to serve the individual, not to make him fit into a standardized program. . . . The individual is the focal point and all the activities of the school are weighed and evaluated in the light of their possibilities for contributing to the orientation and upbuilding of each student.[9]

Guidance, a more specific term than *personnel work*, seems to refer to the particular services that are deemed necessary as a practical application of the personnel point of view within educational institutions. Historically, the rise of the guidance movement in American education is commonly attributed to the work of Frank Parsons and his "Breadwinners Institute" at Boston in the first decade of the twentieth century. Although Parsons was primarily interested in vocational aspects of guidance, the influence of many other factors has broadened the modern concept of guidance to a notable degree. Thus Traxler avers that our present day guidance movement has sprung from several divergent and highly dissimilar sources which he enumerates as follows: philanthropy or humanitarianism; religion; mental hygiene; social change; and the measurement movement.[10] It is because of this fact that Traxler finds the present confusion in guidance literature understandable. "When the guidance movement is seen as resulting from so many influ-

---

[8]Andrew Crawford, "Educational Personnel Work," *Personnel Journal*, X (1932), 405-10.

[9]Charles E. Germane and Edith G. Germane, *Personnel Work in High School* (Chicago: Silver Burdett Co., 1941), p. 20.

[10]Arthur Traxler, *Techniques of Guidance* (New York: Harper Brothers, 1945), p. 4.

ences there can be little wonder that the field of guidance is confused and uncertain."[11]

The concept of guidance in this study is the one proposed in the Evaluative Criteria of the Cooperative Study of Secondary School Standards. This is stated in clear and objective language on the "G" Blank:

Guidance services, . . . should be thought of as organized activities designed to give systematic aid to pupils in solving their problems and in making adjustment to the various situations which they must meet. These activities should assist each pupil in knowing himself as an individual and as a member of society; in making the most of his strengths and in correcting or compensating for weaknesses that interfere with his progress; in learning about occupations so that he may intelligently plan and prepare, in whole or in part, for a career; in learning about educational opportunities available to him; and in discovering and developing creative leisure and interests.[12]

To make this concept of guidance practical it is necessary that there should be an overall plan, specifying the areas of guidance designed to meet the needs of the greatest number of students following a careful diagnosis of those needs. Without this overall plan the quality of "systematic aid" is lost and the guidance service becomes haphazard and ineffective. This concept of guidance is admittedly comprehensive and demands the cooperation of the entire school staff for both the formal and informal rendering of the necessary aid.

Thus understood guidance includes all practical measures that are within the competence of the school, saving the prior rights of the family and the Church, to help students meet the pressing needs of everyday life. It includes a comprehensive testing program for aptitude and achievement, personality adjustment, attitudes, and interests; a program for group guidance; systematic cumulative records and home reports; diagnostic health services; follow-up and placement services for out-of-school youth, both graduate and non-graduate; and at the center of all, ample provision, in personnel and time, for the individual counseling of all students.

[11]*Ibid.*, p. 6.
[12]*Evaluative Criteria*, "G" Blank," Cooperative Study of Secondary School Standards (Washington, D. C., 1951), p. 221.

THE STATEMENT OF THE PROBLEM 11

The term *Counseling* seems to be more limited than either *personnel work* or *guidance*. This has not always been the concept of counseling used in personnel and guidance work.

In the past counseling was accepted in a very broad sense, as Wrenn points out:

> Cawley[13] stated that counselors are to assist in personalizing the educational program of students and coordinating for the student the various personnel services of the institution. When used in this sense, counseling means the whole of individualized personnel work.[14]

This broad interpretation of counseling seems to have been the cause of some of the confusion which is now observed in personnel and guidance literature. If counseling is accepted in this broad sense it is difficult to distinguish it from the other two concepts. As a consequence it is also difficult to arrive at a clear notion of the formalities involved in the process of counseling.

In recent years there has been a noticeable effort by educationists and psychologists to limit the term and to emphasize counseling as the central phase of personnel and guidance work. Wrenn takes cognizance of this trend and accepts the more specific meaning of counseling. He states:

> In contrast to this over-all meaning of the term a more recent point of view would consider counseling as only one phase of individualized personnel work. . . . The discussion of counseling in this section will assume the specific rather than the generalized connotation.[15]

Wrenn has expressed a similar preference for the specific view of counseling in at least two previous publications.[16, 17] In one of these he attempts to define counseling in its educational application and to distinguish it from other educational

[13]William H. Cawley, "A Preface to the Principles of Student Counseling," *Educational Record*, XVIII (1937), 217-34.

[14]Gilbert Wrenn, "General Counseling Procedures," *Encyclopedia of Educational Research*. Edited by Walter S. Monroe (1941), p. 269.

[15]*Ibid.*, p. 269.

[16]Gilbert Wrenn, "Counseling with Students," *Thirty-Seventh Yearbook* National Society for the Study of Education, (Chicago: University of Chicago Press, 1938), pp. 119-43.

[17]Gilbert Wrenn, "The Interview," *Review of Educational Research*, IX (1939), 201-204, 242-43.

practices. For this purpose he selects four general characteristics of counseling: its personal nature; implication of greater maturity and understanding in the counselor; the mutual consideration of a problem or situation; and the goal of the process, i.e., to help others make adjustments, to develop ability to see alternatives and to act upon them, to clarify muddy thinking, to resolve dependent attitudes, and to face reality in their own lives. He then weaves these elements into a definition which he thinks will distinguish counseling from formal teaching and indicate its specialized nature. He states his definition in this manner:

> Counseling is a personal and dynamic relationship between two people who approach a mutually defined problem with mutual consideration for each other to the end that the younger, or less mature, or more troubled of the two is aided to a self-determined resolution of his problem.[18]

Williamson emphasizes the distinctive character of counseling in the educational field by the use of the term *clinical* which he applies both to the professional counselor and to the process.[19] Clinical counseling is for him "one of the basic types of personnel work with individual students."[20] Though Williamson and Darley divided the work of the clinical counselor into six steps, one of these steps seems to be in substantial agreement with the definition of Wrenn noted above.[21] The fifth step Williamson calls "counseling (treatment)" and explains it in the following way: "Counseling refers to the steps taken by the student and the counselor to bring about adjustment and readjustment.[22]

The definition of counseling that Rogers proposes in the *Review of Educational Research* does not seem to differ radically

---

[18]Wrenn, *Thirty-Seventh Yearbook*, p. 121.

[19]Edmund G. Williamson, *How to Counsel Students* (New York: McGraw-Hill, 1939), pp. 36-61.

[20]Edmund G. Williamson, *Counseling Adolescents* (New York: McGraw-Hill, 1950), p. 51.

[21]Edmund G. Williamson and John G. Darley, *Student Personnel Work* (New York: McGraw-Hill, 1937), pp. 168-83.

[22]Williamson, *Counseling Adolescents*, p. 101.

from the ideas of Wrenn and Williamson as expressed above.[23] Ruth Strang has expressed a similar notion of counseling in one of her books.[24] Bordin seems to follow the same trend when he suggests that counseling be defined as

> ... an interview relationship between two persons in which one person accepts the responsibility for defining the nature of that relationship and its process with the expectation that it will lead to increased happiness for the other person.[25]

Though there are slight differences in each of these definitions of counseling it seems clear from the common elements noted that there are greater similarities than differences. It is probably true, as Arbuckle points out, that, although there may be slight differences of opinion as to the exact "definitions, function, and techniques of counseling," most clinical counselors will agree that it is a "person-to-person relationship and that its basic concern is human development."[26]

Consequent to and in view of the above discussion, it seems reasonable that the definition and specific meaning of counseling as proposed by Wrenn be adopted as the working definition of this study. This definition has the common elements that are apparently accepted by most counselors and will therefore serve to limit this study to a specific field. With slight modification this view of counseling may be restated as follows:

> Counseling is a personal and dynamic *interview* relationship between two people who approach a mutually defined problem, with mutual consideration for each other to the end that the younger, or less mature, or more troubled of the two is aided to a self-determined resolution of his problem.[27]

---

[23]Carl R. Rogers, "Counseling," *Review of Educational Research*, XV (1945), 155.

[24]Ruth Strang, *The Role of the Teacher in Personnel Work* (New York: Columbia University Press, 1946), p. 252.

[25]Edmund S. Bordin, "Counseling Points of View," *Trends in Student Personnel Work*, edited by Edmund Williamson (Minneapolis: University of Minnesota Press, 1949), p. 121.

[26]Dugold S. Arbuckle, *Teacher Counseling* (Cambridge: Addison-Wesley Press, 1950), p. 178.

[27]Wrenn, *Thirty-Seventh Yearbook*, p. 119. (Italics added.)

While it is recognized that the term *interview*, which has been made explicit, has a variety of purposes, and applications, and functions in many other situations involving human relations, it is placed here in the definition of counseling as the general tool or technique of the process which serves to specify counseling as the heart of a more complete guidance program. It is this concept of counseling that is the subject of the present study.

Thus *counseling* is considered as the one phase of individualized *personnel work*, the heart and center of an organized *guidance program*, in which the counselor attempts to aid the student through personal interview to a better insight into his problems, decisions, and possible actions by providing him with an opportunity for more objective and adequate consideration of these factors.

Sources of Investigation

As was indicated in the formulation of the problem the sources of this investigation will be in two general fields: first, the field of counseling and guidance; second, the field of scholastic moral science. An awareness of the vastness of both of these fields shows the necessity of selection. The principle of selection will be the representative works of those who are considered, for various reasons, to be representative authorities in their respective fields. The danger inherent in such selection is recognized but overruled in the cause of practicality.

In the counseling field there is the twofold division of the traditional and the new schools of thought. The following authors and books have been selected as representative of the traditional school:

Arthur Jones, a Professor of Education at the University of Pennsylvania, whose text *Principles of Guidance* originally published in 1930 and revised in 1945 has been widely used in this field.[28]

Ruth Strang, a Professor of Education at Teachers College, Columbia University, has written prodigiously in guidance and

[28]Arthur Jones, *Principles of Guidance* (New York: McGraw-Hill, 1945), p. 592.

counseling as well as in related fields. Her revised and enlarged edition of *Counseling Technics in College and Secondary Schools* has been selected as representing her views.[29]

Edmund G. Williamson, Dean of Students and Professor of Psychology at the University of Minnesota, a man of vast experience in the practical work of counseling. His revision of Part 1 of *How to Counsel Students*[30] now published under the title, *Counseling Adolescents*, has been chosen because as the author states in the *Preface*, this revision centers around a "new formulation of the broadened role of counseling in education."[31]

Robert H. Mathewson, Director of the Guidance Center, Cambridge, Massachusetts, conducted under the auspices of Boston College, Boston University, Harvard University, Institute of Technology, Northeastern University, and Tufts College, has been selected because of his efforts to construct a "framework of fundamental theory which may be useful in evaluating current guidance practice. . . ." This he has done in his book, *Guidance Policy and Practice*.[32]

As representative of the new or client-centered school of thought, it seems reasonable to center this investigation on the work of Carl R. Rogers, Professor of Psychology at the University of Chicago, formerly of Ohio State University, and the Director of the Rochester Guidance Center. His book, *Counseling and Psychotherapy*,[33] contained the most complete statement of the non-directive view until recently when he published a new book entitled, *Client-Centered Therapy*.[34] Other

[29]Ruth Strang, *Counseling Technics in College and Secondary Schools* (New York: Harper and Brothers, 1949), p. 302.

[30]Edmund G. Williamson, *How to Counsel Students* (New York: McGraw-Hill, 1939), p. 562.

[31]Edmund G. Williamson, *Counseling Adolescents* (New York: McGraw-Hill, 1950), p. 548.

[32]Robert H. Mathewson, *Guidance Policy and Practice* (New York: Harper and Brothers, 1949), p. 291.

[33]Carl R. Rogers, *Counseling and Psychotherapy* (New York: Houghton Mifflin Co., 1942), p. 450.

[34]Carl R. Rogers, *Client-Centered Therapy* (New York: Houghton Mifflin Co., 1951), p. 560.

works of Rogers, in both book and periodical form, as well as the writings of his disciples, William U. Snyder, Arthur W. Combs, and others, will be cited where clarifications and developments of the original theory have been made.

As a representative authority in the field of scholastic moral science St. Thomas Aquinas has been selected. His writings grouped under the title of *Opera Omnia*, which in one edition (Vives) number thirty-four volumes, and the approved commentators of the Thomistic school, will be followed for the critical evaluation of the problem.[35, 36, 37]

---

[35] St. Thomas Aquinas, *Opera Omnia* (Paris: Vives Edition, 1872-1880).

[36] St. Thomas Aquinas, *Summa Theologica* (Rome: Leonine Edition, 1888-1906).

[37] St. Thomas Aquinas, *Summa Theologica* (New York: Benziger Brothers, Inc., 1947).

CHAPTER II

CURRENT SCHOOLS OF COUNSELING

THE TRADITIONAL SCHOOL

Arthur Jones

The first representative of the traditional school of counseling to be considered is Arthur Jones, of the University of Pennsylvania. His views of the nature, aims, and methods of counseling have been gathered from the revised edition of his text, *Principles of Guidance*.[1] This book has been a standard text in the field of guidance for many years. It was originally published in 1930.

Jones describes counseling as a general method of guidance[2] but because of its intimate sound would limit counseling to the intimate heart-to-heart talk between teacher and pupil.[3] He believes that it is the most intimate and vital part of a guidance program[4] and involves the clearing up of problems by discussion.[5] Counseling is distinctly an educational process and resembles somewhat the manner used by Socrates.[6]

For the specific nature of counseling Jones adapts a definition of Wrenn which he believes expresses in condensed form the essence of the activity and the relationship. He states:

> Counseling is a personal and dynamic relationship between two individuals, one of whom is older, or more experienced, or wiser than the other, who approaches a more or less well defined problem of the younger, or less experienced, or less wise, with mutual consideration for each other to the end that the problem may be more clearly defined, and that the one who has the problem may be helped to a self-determined solution of it.[7]

[1] Arthur Jones, *Principles of Guidance* (New York: McGraw-Hill, 1945), p. 593.
[2] *Ibid.*, p. 265.
[3] *Ibid.*, p. 268.
[4] *Ibid.*, p. 268.
[5] *Ibid.*, p. 269.
[6] *Ibid.*, p. 269.
[7] *Ibid.*, p. 269.

Jones concludes his consideration of the specific nature of counseling with the observation that it is an activity where all the facts are gathered together, all the experiences of the student are focused upon the problem to be solved by him, and where he is given direct and personal help in arriving at a solution but it is not solving the problem for him.[8]

As the most intimate and vital part of the guidance program, counseling shares in the common purpose of all guidance which Jones believes to be aiding the individual to make wise choices, adjustments, and interpretations in connection with critical situations in his life through direct assistance.[9] A more ultimate aim of counseling he expresses thus: "Counseling should aim at the progressive development of the individual to solve his own problems unassisted."[10]

In the definition of counseling which Jones has proposed he presents the proximate aim of counseling as the clearer definition of problems so that the one who has the problems may be helped to a self-determined solution of them.[11]

In the discussion of methods of counseling Jones limits himself to the consideration of the *interview* which he considers as an essential element in clinical methods, though he believes that counseling can be very effectively accomplished in quite informal and brief conversations.[12]

He proposes that the counselor should prepare for the interview by bringing together and reviewing all available data on the pupil so that it will be possible to follow up all clues, understand and interpret the statements of the pupil in terms of this background,[13] and formulate tentative problems, objectives, and plans for the interview. At the same time the counselor should keep an open mind regarding the problems as the interview develops and accept the individual as he is.[14] Each interview should be considered as a step in the process of guiding the pupil and should be planned with due regard for the past and the future.[15]

---

[8]*Ibid.*, p. 270.
[9]*Ibid.*, p. 80.
[10]*Ibid.*, p. 270.
[11]*Ibid.*, p. 269.

[12]*Ibid.*, p. 272.
[13]*Ibid.*, p. 273.
[14]*Ibid.*, p. 274.
[15]*Ibid.*, p. 274.

As to the steps of the process of counseling Jones presents the *Techniques of Interviewing* which he quotes in full from the *Manual for Teachers and Other Guidance Workers* by Margaret E. Bennet.[16] She had adapted them in part from *Guide to Effective Interviewing* by Ella M. Stubbs, Clinical Psychologist, Pasadena City Schools. The steps are ten in number and may be summarized as follows:

Establish rapport. Feelings of friendliness, security, and mutual confidence are essential and should be established before the serious work of the interview begins.[17]

Interviews should avoid evidences of fatigue, pressure, irritation, or lack of ease, and desirably should be free of these, as well as their manifestations.

Greetings should be cordial, businesslike, without display of authority, and should reveal concentrated interest in the student's problems.

The major purposes of the interview should be mutually formulated early in the interview.

Keep control of the interview, but guide it unobtrusively, working steadily toward the objective without dawdling, and confine discussion to issues at hand.

Avoid critical attitudes and moralizing. Do nothing to undermine the interviewee's self-respect. Even if his behavior is disapproved, he himself should be accepted. Neither ridicule nor condemn, but try to understand.

Help the student come to grips with his problems, do his own thinking, reach his own conclusions, and change his own feelings and behavior. See that his thinking is challenged and that he has the needed facts and insights to make sound judgments.

Before the end of the interview, the student should have drawn up a reasonable plan of action for the immediate and remote future. This plan may be chiefly one of further study, but it is desirable to have some specific, concrete activities mapped out.[18]

The student should leave the interview with the feeling of having had a satisfying and genuinely helpful experience.

No interview is complete before salient points are recorded.[19]

---

[16]Margaret E. Bennet, *Manual for Teachers and Other Guidance Workers* (Pasadena: Board of Education, 1941), pp. 100-02.
[17]Jones, *op. cit.*, p. 274.
[18]*Ibid.*, p. 275.
[19]*Ibid.*, p. 276.

Jones seems to consider these recommendations sufficient to aid the counselor in meeting the needs of the student. He maintains that the process of counseling is designed to help the student in his need which may include the interpretation of information, some listening and advising, help in the mobilization of aids not easily accessible, assistance in recognizing unrecognized but existent problems and the understanding of recognized problems, or the promotion of constructive action and help in major maladjustments.[20]

Jones takes cognizance of the non-directive proposals of Rogers but concludes that they are indicated only when serious emotional disturbances are evidenced. He states his position:

> It is, at best, only one of a number of ways or avenues through which we may help the maladjusted person. The work of the school counselor should include all types of maladjustments, all kinds of problems, whether severe emotional disturbances are involved or not.[21]

Ruth Strang

The second representative of the traditional school of counseling is Ruth Strang, a well known authority in the field of guidance and counseling. She is a Professor of Education at Teachers College, Columbia University. Her revised and enlarged edition of *Counseling Technics in Colleges and Secondary Schools* has been selected as the source of her mature views on the nature, aims, and methods of counseling.[22]

Strang describes counseling in general as a face-to-face relationship in which a counselor helps a person to gain insight, new orientation, a more acceptable self-concept, better ways of thinking about problems and relationships, and new technics of living.[23] It may range from rather superficial advice-giving to helping the individual to gain genuine insight into his attitudes, behavior and relationships.[24] Counseling at its best is an art by which a person is helped to understand himself, his relation

[20] *Ibid.*, p. 272.
[21] *Ibid.*, p. 279.
[22] Ruth Strang, *Counseling Technics in College and Secondary Schools* (New York: Harper and Brothers, 1949), p. 302.
[23] *Ibid.*, p. 7.
[24] *Ibid.*, p. 8.

to others and the world in which he lives, and it is to be considered as a learning experience for the student.[25] It should not be problem-centered or counselor-centered, or technique-centered, but the process should be centered on the individual-in-his-environment.[26]

Strang defines counseling specifically in the following way:
Counseling is a face-to-face relationship in which a person who needs help in developing his most acceptable self, or in solving personal problems is given the opportunity to gain insight by thinking through the situation himself in an accepting atmosphere. The counselor may facilitate the process by supplying information and making changes in the environment indicated in the course of counseling.[27]

There are five essentials to be observed in the process. The first is the relationship between counselor and counselee, the heart of the process,[28] in which the counselee has a sense of responsibility for using resources within himself to help himself, while the counselor contributes warmth, responsiveness, and acceptance of the person as he is and can become in the growth experience.[29]

The second essential is the psychological "atmosphere" of permissiveness, acceptance, and freedom created by the counselor to help the client explore and express his feelings, gain a new perception of the situation, be himself, gather courage to face feelings with no need to hide or justify them, and be stimulated to use more mature ways of meeting the demands of the present.[30]

In the third essential, "facilitation of counselee effort," the counselor conveys his understanding of the student by reflecting his more positive and significant feelings, emotions, and ideas, and makes acccessible needed information which the counselee uses as he wishes.[31]

The fourth essential, "attention to adjustment in life situations," extends the work of the counselor beyond the counseling situation to the environment and provides needed experience for good adjustment in life.[32]

[25]*Ibid.*, p. 15.
[26]*Ibid.*
[27]*Ibid.*, p. 11.
[28]*Ibid.*, p. 12.
[29]*Ibid.*, p. 13.
[30]*Ibid.*
[31]*Ibid.*
[32]*Ibid.*, p. 14.

The fifth essential, "the follow-up," is necessary for the evaluation of the counseling process as the success of counseling cannot be judged solely by what goes on in the interview.[33]

Strang states the ultimate aim of counseling in social terms, an aspect of counseling which she thinks has been generally neglected in spite of the fact that counseling is a potent means of building better people and a better world through its direct influence on social attitudes. She states, "The aim of counseling is self-realization for a social purpose."[34]

This ultimate aim of counseling is attained through the proximate aims of the process which include helping the individual to understand what he can and should do to strengthen his best qualities, to handle his difficulties rationally rather than being driven by unconscious forces, to find suitable channels for his emotions, and to move toward his more acceptable self which implies a concern for the welfare of all.[35]

Discussing methods of counseling in general Strang believes it important that the counselor should not concentrate on technics, or use them mechanically lest they interfere with the essential warm relationship between the counselor and the counselee.[36] The former must always be aware of the dynamics of the process and use any technic or instrument that will help the individual to understand, accept, or realize his most acceptable self at any given moment.[37] Analysis and synthesis of information[38] gathered from observation, testing, daily schedule, and physical examination,[39] leading to diagnosis of cause and dynamics of the individual's behavior seem essential to attain the goal of the process.[40]

Strang centers on the interview as the specific method of counseling where all information about the individual becomes more complete, clear, and accurate.[41] It is the heart of the counseling process, to which other technics are contributory. Its essential features is the dynamic face-to-face relationship, a learning experience valuable in and for itself, both to the

[33]Ibid.
[34]Ibid., p. 15.
[35]Ibid.
[36]Ibid., p. 29.
[37]Ibid., p. 30.
[38]Ibid., p. 21.
[39]Ibid., p. 19.
[40]Ibid., p. 27.
[41]Ibid., p. 19.

counselor and the counselee, through which the latter is helped to develop insights leading to self-realization. More than other technics the success of the interview depends on the personality of the counselor, his respect for people, his faith in their innate abilities,[42] and his understanding of the purpose and nature of the process.[43]

Strang discusses the steps of the process from preplanning to "post mortem," which do not always seem to be perfectly discrete. These may be summarized as follows:

The setting for the interview is characterized by genuine friendliness, acceptance, and informality. Reputation of the counselor for giving a "square deal," recognizing the student's point of view, and constructive help in joint solution of problems, is the most important single factor for success.[44]

Background information from cumulative records, case studies, knowledge of student problems, and understanding of the nature of the adjustment are all equally important.[45]

Student comes to the interview of his own volition, indicating that he is ready to accept responsibility for working on his problem. If this is not the case the counselor should recognize feelings, explain the nature of the counseling process, and try to build rapport.[46]

Structuring the interview consists in securing the client's cooperation by explaining the counseling process, what is expected of the client, and his responsibility for using the available resources.[47]

Gaining rapport. Recognize individual differences and adapt approach accordingly. Thinking and feeling with the client, empathy and sympathy, indicate when to reflect feelings, when to be silent, and when to interpret.[48, 49]

Establishing a counseling relationship. A beneficial relationship grows out of the counselor's feelings about people, his respect for human beings, acceptance of them as they are and can become, faith in their ability to work out their salvation, resulting in a warm, accepting understanding which is personal but not involved, objective but not cold or disinterested.[50]

Recognizing, accepting, reflecting, and clarifying the counselee's feelings. Listen, accept, and reflect the client's nega-

[42] *Ibid.*, p. 100.
[43] *Ibid.*, p. 113.
[44] *Ibid.*, p. 121.
[45] *Ibid.*, p. 122.
[46] *Ibid.*, p. 123.
[47] *Ibid.*, p. 124.
[48] *Ibid.*, p. 125.
[49] *Ibid.*, p. 126.
[50] *Ibid.*, p. 127.

tive feelings naturally expressed in the first part of the interview, and help clarify views and perhaps perceive his situation in a new light. Indicate acceptance by bodily position, facial expression, or by gestures, but the client is more certain of acceptance if the counselor rephrases feelings accurately. The skillful counselor does not merely repeat words nor, usually, intellectual content but expresses feelings in words which often help to clarify them. Reflection of feelings has perhaps been overemphasized as a technic. If the counselor is too intent and anxious about it he may block the free communication which is the most essential part of the process and the client may get the impression of prying into his private world.[51, 52]

Interpretation is not sharply distinct from reflection of feelings. It is not easy, yet it is often needed to stimulate the client to explore further, for without it the counselee may remain on a superficial level of self-understanding and not make progress. Premature interpretations may not be so serious as some counselors believe, because the individual tends to ignore them if he is not ready.[53, 54, 55]

Developing insight that leads to desirable changes of behavior is the major goal of interviewing. Any technic that helps the client clarify and understand his feelings and conflicts should lead to insight. Any technic that encourages the counselee to use insights in real life situations will help make insights functional. Mere acceptance of feelings will not achieve this end; in fact there is danger that the counselee will build a picture of himself out of line with reality and with the criteria of social acceptability.[56]

Putting insights to work. The student often needs help in translating insights into real life experiences. The successful counselor is resourceful, finding suitable educational opportunities, jobs, or recreational groups, thinks of ingenious ways out of difficult situations, though he is most happy if the student can do these things for himself so that the counselor need only reinforce the plan by a word of approval. It is frequently necessary to reduce environmental pressures so that the student can handle them.[57, 58]

Encouraging continuation of therapy between interviews. Most growth takes place outside or between the interviews, when the thinking begun in the interview is continued and

[51] *Ibid.*, p. 129.
[52] *Ibid.*, p. 130.
[53] *Ibid.*
[54] *Ibid.*, p. 131.
[55] *Ibid.*, p. 132.
[56] *Ibid.*
[57] *Ibid.*, p. 133.
[58] *Ibid.*, p. 134.

insight gained in the interview are put to work in daily living.[59]

Terminating the contact. Counseling should end with a mutual recognition that independence is a healthy step toward growth. The termination should not be abrupt, but a natural stage in the process, leaving the way open for the client's return if he feels in need of further help. Follow-up is made to determine whether the client has made adjustment in life situation.[60]

Keeping records of interview. Records are needed for service purposes and research. Sound recordings made with the client's consent are obviously superior to note taking, as they make possible verbatim records, preserve the tone of voice, inflections, pauses, and leave the counselor free to concentrate on the listening process.[61, 62]

Edmund G. Williamson

The third representative of the traditional school of counseling to be studied in this investigation is Edmund G. Williamson, Dean of Students and Professor of Psychology at the University of Minnesota. Williamson has revised Part 1 of an earlier book[63] with its emphasis upon clinical counseling and now "centers his work around a new formulation of the broadened role of counseling in education."[64]

Williamson describes counseling in general as one of the personalized and individualized[65] fundamental techniques[66] of assisting the individual to achieve both immediate personal adjustment and prepare for remote and adult adjustment through a one-to-one relationship in learning.[67] Counseling is both a supplementary and alternative method of facilitating adjustment and removing obstacles to learning.[68] It is a methodology of assisting adolescents in developing their personalities[69] in the transition from childhood to adulthood.[70] Broadly conceived

---

[59] *Ibid.*
[60] *Ibid.*, p. 135.
[61] *Ibid.*
[62] *Ibid.*, p. 136.
[63] Edmund G. Williamson, *How to Counsel Students* (New York: McGraw-Hill, 1939), p. 562.
[64] *Ibid., Counseling Adolescents* (New York: McGraw-Hill, 1950), p. vii.
[65] *Ibid.*, p. 2.
[66] *Ibid.*, p. 3.
[67] *Ibid.*, p. 4.
[68] *Ibid.*, p. 18.
[69] *Ibid.*, p. 28.
[70] *Ibid.*, p. 29.

counseling is a life adjustment type of teacher-student learning experience.[71]

Williamson distinguishes clinical counseling from ordinary counseling, recognizing that while the former is only one of the several specialized fields dealing with personal problems, it is the basic type for work with individual students. It often serves to coordinate and focus the findings of other types of workers.[72]

The essential function of clinical counselors is to provide adequate diagnosis which will serve as a dependable basis for counseling with complex and difficult problems beyond the competency of teachers and untrained advisors.[73] Clinical counseling embraces six steps: analysis, synthesis, diagnosis, prognosis, counseling (treatment), and follow-up.[74] It differs from ordinary counseling in the collection of more exhaustive data, the more critical review of these data, and the diagnosing from relevant and irrelevant data of a more valid, meaningful, and complete interpretation.[75] It is particularly in this last respect, the interpretation of data, that clinical counseling differs most from ordinary counseling.[76]

In actual practice the clinical counselor uses a flexible procedure, and the six steps of clinical counseling do not necessarily follow in sequence. Every student must be dealt with at a different pace to produce the optimum results.[77] Thus the process of counseling frequently reverses and reorders itself.[78]

Analysis refers to the collection, by counselor and student, of dependable data necessary for an adequate understanding of the student before he can be effectively counseled.[79] Williamson discusses six general tools used in analysis as sources of information: cumulative records, the interview, time distribution form, autobiography, anecdotes, and psychological tests.[80] He concludes that these analytic procedures are indispensable if the counselor and the student are to arrive at a diagnosis of

[71]*Ibid.*, p. 110.
[72]*Ibid.*, p. 51.
[73]*Ibid.*, p. 75.
[74]*Ibid.*, p. 101.
[75]*Ibid.*, p. 102.
[76]*Ibid.*
[77]*Ibid.*
[78]*Ibid.*, p. 103.
[79]*Ibid.*, p. 127.
[80]*Ibid.*, p. 135-50.

the student and if counseling is to result in appropriate and satisfying adjustment.[81]

In clinical counseling and diagnosis, the opposite of analyzing, the counselor and the student search for a pattern of consistency in the data collected with a view to the past, present, and future adjustment.[82] Diagnosis is a cooperative undertaking with the student assuming major responsibility in understanding himself.[83] It involves three major steps: identifying the problem, discovering causes, and indicating counseling treatment, therapy, or other steps to satisfactory adjustment.[84] As an art it is defined as the evaluation, interpretation, and prognostic signification of data.[85] Williamson concludes that counseling will increase in usefulness only as its techniques of diagnosis becomes more accurate and as its workers use these techniques more skillfully.[86]

Williamson begins his consideration of the *Techniques of Counseling* with what seems to be his specific definition of counseling. He states: "Counseling is that part of personnel work in which a counselor helps the client to marshal his own resources, the resources of an institution and of the community, to assist the client to achieve the optimum adjustment of which he is capable."[87] He then distinguishes five different types of relationships and services involving counselee and counselor for which the term "counseling" is used in his book. These are a relationship of guided learning toward self-understanding; certain kinds of reeducation or relearning needed for life adjustment, e.g., reading habits or techniques of working and living; personalized assistance in understanding and use of general semantics in daily living; a repertoire of therapeutic or curative techniques and relationships leading to insight and the end of counseling; and therapeutic catharsis followed by some form of reeducation.[88]

Recognizing that each of these has common as well as unique features,[89] and that in real life there are numerous interrela-

[81] *Ibid.*, p. 150.
[82] *Ibid.*, p. 178.
[83] *Ibid.*, p. 180.
[84] *Ibid.*, p. 185.
[85] *Ibid.*, p. 207.
[86] *Ibid.*, p. 208.
[87] *Ibid.*, p. 209.
[88] *Ibid.*, p. 210.
[89] *Ibid.*

tionships and combinations of these five types of counseling, Williamson chooses to stress the first three types.[90]

Williamson then formulates what seems to be another descriptive definition or "concept of counseling,"[91] which clearly manifests his preferred concept of the nature of counseling and how it is to be understood. He states, "Counseling is a *generalized method of learning to deal with all kinds of situation.*"[92] This concept he explains in the following way: as cause and effect operate in all areas of life, the client needs to learn the methods of analysis, diagnosis, prognosis, counseling, and follow-up with respect to all phases of life, for counseling methodology, with certain adaptations to diferences in situations is applicable throughout life. Thus he concludes, the tendency to restrict counseling to insight therapy does not exhaust its rich possibilities as a general method of problem solving.[93]

Williamson, in discussing counseling in general, proposes the ultimate aim of counseling in the following way: "Counseling is one of several fundamental techniques of assisting the individual not only to achieve immediate personal adjustment but also prepare for remote and adult adjustment.[94] In another context he states the ultimate aim of counseling in terms of the dominant objective of counseling as "the optimum development of the individual as a whole person and not only with respect to his intellectual training."[95] In the same context he maintains that counseling aims to assist "clients . . . achieve optimum personal development of their potentialities."[96] He adds a social aspect to the ultimate aim when he states the results of effective counseling. "Effective counseling will result in immediate or delayed adjustments (successes) which are both personally satisfying and socially satisfactory."[97]

Williamson speaks of the proximate aim of the counseling process as assisting the client to develop self-directing skills and insights as a basic part of his emerging individuality.[98] The process is designed to offer sympathetic and skillful aid to cli-

[90]*Ibid.*, p. 211.
[91]*Ibid.*
[92]*Ibid.*, p. 213.
[93]*Ibid.*
[94]*Ibid.*, p. 4.
[95]*Ibid.*, p. 25.
[96]*Ibid.*, p. 27.
[97]*Ibid.*, p. 222.
[98]*Ibid.*, p. 23.

ents in learning the ways and means to continued growth and effective living with maximum client initiative, responsibility, and participation.[99] The purpose of diagnosis and counseling is to see that the client perceives the interrelationships of these methods and processes as the *"initial steps in a life-time sequence"* of adjustment and readjustment. Williamson contends that counseling understood as a generalized method of life adjustment[100] is not ordered only to therapy and insight, and to the confirmation of choices or information about opportunities, but also to "a basic understanding and skill in using the methods of analysis, diagnosis, and counseling."[101] His position is clear in this statement:

> It is a magnificent contribution to his life to aid him in gaining present day insight into his emotional conflicts, in dissipating his repressions and releasing his damned-up emotional energies. But it is even more of a counseling contribution to aid him in so conducting the future adjustments that a minimum of maladaptive repressions recur.[102]

Turning to counseling methods in general, Williamson distinguishes and discusses briefly five general methods or categories of counseling techniques:[103] forcing conformity is ill advised but conformity is a very common practice in our culture; change of environment must be made from time to time for all students;[104] selecting appropriate environment or blocking out certain parts;[105] assisting client to learn needed skills;[106] changing attitudes to facilitate a harmonious balance between needs and demands of environment.[107] These five classes of techniques are found in all problem areas and not merely in the field of emotional difficulties.[108]

Williamson maintains there are no standard techniques in either diagnosing or counseling, as techniques are specific to different problems and different situations. In clinical practice flexibility, adaption, and modification are characteristic of the counselor's application of general procedures to particular

[99]*Ibid.*, p. 24.
[100]*Ibid.*, p. 213.
[101]*Ibid.*, p. 215.
[102]*Ibid.*, p. 213.
[103]*Ibid.*, p. 215.
[104]*Ibid.*, p. 216.
[105]*Ibid.*
[106]*Ibid.*
[107]*Ibid.*, p. 217.
[108]*Ibid.*, p. 215.

students and problems,[109] and the *"effective counselor is the one who adapts his techniques of advising to the personality of the student."*[110]

Specifically, Williamson focuses on the personal interview following diagnosis as the obvious and most effective means of accomplishing the counseling function.[111] As the counselor should be prepared to assist the student to solve, choose, master, learn, and deal with the situations of a wide variety,[112] he must have a repertoire of specific techniques from which he selects those appropriate to the nature of the client's problem and the other features of the situation. However, this is not to be considered "an electic concept of counseling."[113]

He classifies and discusses the techniques or steps of the counseling interview under five headings. These are presented in summary:

Establishing rapport. There are no general rules to fit all situations. The reputation of the counselor for competence, kindliness, respect for individuality, for keeping confidences is essential. The personal touch of the counselor, and the feeling of personal understanding manifested are important. Counselor must remain personal in manner and impersonal in his interest.[114, 115]

Cultivating Self-Understanding. The counselor assists student to understand himself, advises what to do, or assists in planning next step. To be effective student must have an enlightened understanding of his own assets and liabilities, and of the implications of diagnosis. Counselor translates technical facts from analysis with which he has familiarized himself before the interview, asks questions, watches the reactions of the student, and directs the conversation accordingly.[116, 117, 118]

Advising or Planning a Program of Action. Counselor begins advising at the point of student's understanding, listing phases of diagnosis for and against the point of reference, explaining why he advises what he does and the implications for the student's adjustment. Counselor states point of view with *definiteness,* but avoids dogmatic position and reveals

[109]*Ibid.,* p. 220.
[110]*Ibid.,* p. 232.
[111]*Ibid.,* p. 217.
[112]*Ibid.,* p. 219.
[113]*Ibid.,* p. 220.
[114]*Ibid.,* p. 225.
[115]*Ibid.,* p. 226.
[116]*Ibid.,* p. 230.
[117]*Ibid.,* p. 228.
[118]*Ibid.,* p. 229.

to student an attitude of bringing knowledge, experience, and judgment to his assistance, seeking to induce an experimental attitude in student to try out counselor's suggestion and his own ideas.[119, 120, 121]

There are three methods of advising: *direct* advising—counselor frankly states opinion regarding most satisfactory choice, action, or program to be made and followed out by the student; *persuasive* when the case indicates quite definitely that one choice is to be preferred; *explanatory*—explain significance of diagnostic data and point out possible situation in which student's potentialities will prove useful. *This is by all odds the most complete and satisfactory* method but requires more time and many interviews.[122, 123, 124]

Carrying out the plan. Counselor is often able to assist the student directly and referral is unnecessary. Counselor's training and experience determine what type of direct assistance he may provide.[125]

Referral to Other Personnel Workers. When counselor recognizes the need for assistance in diagnosis and advising, he refers the student to specialized sources for information and assistance which he cannot provide. This may be done at any point in his interviewing.[126]

Robert H. Mathewson

The fourth representative of the traditional school of counseling considered in this study is Robert H. Mathewson, Director of the Guidance Center, Cambridge, Massachusetts. It is possible that Mathewson would object to being classified as of the traditional school. He directed his efforts in *Guidance Policy and Practice* to the construction of a "frame work of fundamental theory" for the evaluation of current guidance practice.[127] In his chapter entitled "The Role of the Counselor," he condenses an article that he had published under the same title in the *Harvard Educational Review*.[128] In this he attempts to "delineate the nature of counseling in a reasonable definitive

[119]*Ibid.*, p. 229.
[120]*Ibid.*, p. 230.
[121]*Ibid.*, p. 231.
[122]*Ibid.*, p. 233.
[123]*Ibid.*
[124]*Ibid.*, p. 244.
[125]*Ibid.*, p. 236.
[126]*Ibid.*, p. 237.

[127]Robert H. Mathewson, *Guidance Policy and Practice* (New York: Harper and Brothers, 1949), p. 291.

[128]*Ibid.*, "The Role of the Counselor," *Harvard Educational Review*, XVII (1947), 10-27.

way."[129] In effect his efforts seem to manifest no major differences from the position of Jones and Strang, and only minor differences from Williamson. For this reason he is included in the traditional school.

Mathewson proposes a conception of counseling that is designedly broad that it may cover many different modes of counseling in many different types of institutional situations. He proposes this concept as a convenient way of designating the process for general purposes. This general concept is stated as follows: "Counseling may be thought of as any mode of professional aid extended to the individual through verbal educative means by which the individual is enabled to make improved adjustments and to pursue his individual development more effectively."[130] It seems obvious that this concept of counseling is not the one to "delineate" the nature of counseling unless that delineation consists in the mere recognition that the dominating conception must be an educative one, the attainment of an educative aim by educative means.[131] This concept is not sufficient to distinguish counseling from any other enlightened professional educative practice.

Mathewson, aware of this fact, attempts to arrive at a more specific concept through the analysis of the basic characteristics[132] and related conditions of the process.[133] He arrives at five conclusions which summarize his understanding of the process and the role of the counselor in it.[134] Thus he states: "Counseling may be considered as taking place in any situation where all four fundamental characteristics, and related conditions, are present, and where individual interest is served."[135] On this basis a specific definition of his concept of counseling may be constructed and stated thus: Counseling consists in

> . . . direct personal communication between counselor and client in a professionally controlled and guided cooperative investigation with variant responsibility *to appraise* the individual-environment, *to evaluate,* correlate, and interpret personal and non-personal factors of the problem situation,

[129]*Ibid.*, p. 10.
[130]Mathewson, *Guidance Policy and Practice*, p. 208.
[131]*Ibid.*, p. 207.
[132]*Ibid.*, p. 194.   [134]*Ibid.*
[133]*Ibid.*, p. 208.   [135]*Ibid.*

to offer adjustive, orientational, and developmental aid to the client through verbal, psychological, educative means *for the purpose of increasing* the client's powers of satisfactory self-direction.[136-140] [Italics added.]

Mathewson arrives at this concept of counseling through the study of four basic elements that appear in all counseling situations.[141] These are in brief: personal communication; appraisal of individual-environment; evaluation of case factors; developmental, adjustive, orientational aid.[142] He suggests these attributes because they cover the widest possible range of counseling practices at all age levels and with all types of problems, and permit broad variations in techniques of a trained professional type.[143]

The basis for this synthesis is found in the concept of the problem-situation as a "field," including both participants and all subjective and objective factors which comprise a distinct "situation in itself."[144] This conception attempts to bring out into full view of both participants in the cooperative venture the factors that can be correlated, thought about, and deliberately acted upon.[145] Interviewing, appraisal, and evaluative activities are closely interrelated and while there may be some "structuring" of the counseling situation, the process is seen as a unified, interlocking action, with one factor dependent for weight and meaning upon all the other factors.[146]

The process of counseling is a cooperative enterprise with variant participation of the counselor or the client according to the nature of the total problem situation and the varying needs of the process as it develops.[147] When so conceived, interpretive, informative, or other types of aid introduced by the counselor will be seen as a contribution to joint-action and not as any attempt to dominate the scene.[148]

This view of counseling assumes that the basic process must occur if the problem situation is to be dealt with effectively

[136] *Ibid.*, p. 194.
[137] *Ibid.*, p. 208.
[138] *Ibid.*, p. 194.
[139] *Ibid.*, p. 208.
[140] *Ibid.*, p. 207.
[141] *Ibid.*, p. 194.
[142] *Ibid.*,
[143] *Ibid.*
[144] *Ibid.*, p. 195.
[145] *Ibid.*, p. 196.
[146] *Ibid.*, p. 197.
[147] *Ibid.*
[148] *Ibid.*, p. 199.

and it occurs in direct connection with the counseling situation.[149] It admits the work of all counselors who vary both their own participation and that of the client according to the situation.[150] Such a range of emphasis invariably occurs in the practical performance of counseling.[151]

The interpretations of the counselor are considered co-equal with those of the client and both are treated in an objective manner. The client chooses what he will do as a result of the joint evaluation.[152] The counselor's judgment of his degree of responsibility is not rigidly fixed beforehand nor is it completely arbitrary, but is based on the characteristics of the problem-situation which emphasizes the needs of the client.[153]

The counseling process is neither client-centered nor counselor-centered, but involves cooperative focus on a field with maximum attention to clarification, objectification, and rational consideration of all factors including the subjective data from the client.[154]

The psychological relationship between counselor and client is fundamentally an educational one, but differs from other teacher-learner situations in that the "subject matter" is unknown to both in a very large degree,[155] and is concerned with "internal" psychological factors actually fused in the problem situation. Both must be fellow-investigators of the problem situation.[156] The counselor's role is that of professional and personal socio-psychological interpreter.[157] The client is a cooperative investigator with accent upon the learning phase. He learns about himself, his environment, and about more effective ways of development and adjusting to his environment.[158] The counselor is also a learner, but with the responsibility to deal with the situation so that the maximum learning takes place on the part of the counselee.[159]

Mathewson discusses the ultimate and proximate aims of counseling more fully in his article on "The Role of the Coun-

[149]Ibid.
[150]Ibid.
[151]Ibid., p. 200.
[152]Ibid., p. 201.
[153]Ibid.
[154]Ibid.

[155]Ibid., p. 205.
[156]Ibid.
[157]Ibid., p. 206.
[158]Ibid., p. 207.
[159]Ibid.

selor" than he does in the chapter of his book. In the former writing he expresses the ultimate aim of all counseling in these words: "The ultimate concern of all counseling may thus be expressed as the fullest possible self-development and self-realization of the individual consistent with universally valid social obligations, and moral values."[160] In his book this same idea is expressed with slight modifications as follows: "The highest possible self-realization consistent with social obligations and moral values is the controlling aim."[161]

Mathewson specifies the proximate aim of counseling in a general manner in his article thus:

The . . . aim of the counseling process is to render aid of some sort to the perplexed individual. The different kinds of aid may be classified one way or another; but that they render aid, of an educative psychological nature, is the pre-eminent fact.[162]

This concept of the proximate aim is made more precise in his book under the formality of a means to the ultimate goal.

This aim (*ultimate*) may be effectively pursued by the *free activation of the individual's powers of learning, adjustability, development, and integration, on the level of conscious apprehension and evaluative reasoning*.[163] [Italics added.]

He clarifies this proximate aim of the counseling process by distinguishing and defining the possible aids that may be rendered. These are three in number:

Adjustive: aid to the individual in adjusting in, or to the immediate situation.

Orientational: aid to the individual in analyzing and understanding about himself and his behavior; in perceiving and learning about pertinent factors in the environmental situation, including opportunities for action; and finally, aid in formulating a definite plan of action.

Developmental: aid which extends the adjustive or orientational aspect to the point of indicating specific ways in which the individual may, through educative experience during and beyond the counseling process, develop personal

[160]*Ibid., Harvard Educational Review*, XVII, 23.
[161]*Ibid., Guidance Policy and Practice*, p. 207.
[162]*Ibid., Harvard Educational Review*, XVII, p. 22.
[163]*Ibid., Guidance Policy and Practice*, p. 207.

capabilities for becoming more effectively purposive and self-directive.[164]

Turning to the consideration of the methods of counseling it is well to recall that Mathewson maintains that the counselor accepts an educative function as the heart and core of his work.[165] The counselor always stands between the client and society, interpreting one to the other, as he attempts to help the individual to satisfactory adjustment and self-realization consistent with social realities and universally valid social sanctions and moral values.[166]

Mathewson's concern with the methods of counseling is not as definitive as the other representatives of the traditional school. From his extensive examination of the basic characteristics or attributes of counseling, suggested because they permit broad variations in the use of specific professional techniques,[167] several of his preferred methods can be gathered.

Mathewson, like the others, would center his consideration of methods on the counseling interview. This is clear from the first "essential phase"[168] of the process, the personal, face-to-face relationship which is the *sine qua non of counseling*," usually occuring in a "professionally controlled and guided situation."[169] The usual place for the exercise of the counseling process has the nature of a general method in the counseling interview.

Though he does not specify the steps of counseling processes precisely, the essential phases of counseling and the suggested techniques are indicated. The appraisal of the individual-environment phase is based on the need of the individual for knowledge about himself in relation to the social norm, involving insight into personal motives and values.[170] If the individual possesses all the data he needs to make his subjective interpretations he may be assisted by the permissive or passive techniques of counseling.[171] If these primary data are lacking the information must be conveyed and interpreted by the coun-

[164] *Ibid.*, p. 207.
[165] *Ibid.*, p. 209.
[166] *Ibid.*, p. 210.
[167] *Ibid.*, p. 194.
[168] *Ibid., Harvard Educational Review*, p. 16.
[169] *Ibid.*
[170] *Ibid.*
[171] *Ibid.*

selor.[172] Knowledge from scientific appraisal of personality though rudimentary and uncertain, qualified and conditional, may be used in counseling for the enlightenment of the client because it is one of the basic reasons why individuals come to the counselor for assistance.[173]

The permissive technique may be the most valuable in the analysis and identification of client needs, motivations, and behavioral mechanisms, but in many instances client insight will have to be assisted by counselor interpretations even where the client actually possesses all the facts to arrive at his own evaluation.[174] In many instances the counselor will have to communicate specific information to the client and tell what it means.[175]

The counselor must be expected to possess primary data about future aspects of the problem situation which the individual does not know. He must be directly provided with information, or access to it may be arranged if he is to be helped. Here referral to the sources of information may be the most effective means, but this does not remove the function from the counseling process, it merely transfers part of the responsibility to the client.[176]

In the review and survey of environmental aspects of the problem-situation, knowledge of the situational scene will be necessary on the part of the counselor, information will have to be conveyed, data will have to be interpreted.[177]

The evaluative phase of counseling may be regarded as the crux of the process. At this point all pertinent factors converge for the evaluation and interpretation by the client and counselor. It is perfectly feasible that the client should assume a large, if not the total share of this function. This does not eliminate the function, but the responsibility is merely passed on to the client who has been conditioned to do so by deliberate structure of the counseling process.[178]

If the client assumes part of the responsibility, the counselor's technical knowledge and professional skill will be re-

[172] *Ibid.*, p. 17.
[173] *Ibid.*
[174] *Ibid.*, p. 18.
[175] *Ibid.*
[176] *Ibid.*, p. 19.
[177] *Ibid.*
[178] *Ibid.*, p. 20.

quired to assist the individual to evaluate and correlate pertinent case factors effectively, without undue imposition of his own personality.[179] It is because of the counselor's ability to exercise the evaluative function that his services will be in demand by many clients.

The need for "another view" of the problem-situation is often the basic requirement which makes the services of the counselor valuable, even in those instances in which considerable personal insight exists.[180]

The Non-Directive School

Carl R. Rogers

Carl R. Rogers, Professor of Psychology at the University of Chicago, is the principal representative of the new or non-directive school of counseling. Rogers originally presented his theory of counseling in *Counseling and Psychotherapy*.[181] A later book, *Client-Centered Therapy*,[182] in the words of the editor, "does not replace his earlier" presentation, but rather "supplements, expands, and qualitatively enriches the views expressed" in it.[183] It appears that there have been some refinements and clarifications of the original theory, experimental evidence has been gathered to support it, and various applications of the theory are made in the latter work. The older book still provides certain essential steps of introduction to the basic concepts which are not repeated in the same detail in *Client-Centered Therapy*.[184] Rogers suggests that the development of his own thinking can be observed from the study of *Counseling and Psychotherapy*, "Significant Aspect of Client-Centered Therapy," and his latest work, *Client-Centered Therapy*.[185]

---

[179]*Ibid.*
[180]*Ibid.*
[181]Carl R. Jones, *Counseling and Psychotherapy* (New York: Houghton Mifflin Co., 1942), pp. 44-45.
[182]Carl R. Rogers, *Client-Centered Therapy* (New York: Houghton Mifflin Co., 1951), p. 560.
[183]*Ibid.*, p. viii.
[184]*Ibid.*
[185]*Ibid.*, p. 18.

Rogers uses the terms "interview treatment," "counseling" and "psychotherapy" more or less interchangeably in his early work because they seem to refer to the same basic method of assisting an individual to change his attitudes and behavior through a series of direct contacts between counselor and client.[186] Thus he indicates the general nature of counseling as he understands it. In the review of experimental work on "Counseling" Rogers describes counseling in these words: "The face-to-face situation through which an effort to alter attitudes, choices, and behavior is made."[187]

He presented his specific definition of counseling as the basic hypothesis of his early book under the noteworthy formality of "effective counseling."

> Effective counseling consists of a definitely structured permissive relationship which allows the client to gain an understanding of himself to a degree which enables him to take positive steps in the light of his new orientation.[188]

This specific definition of counseling is elaborated somewhat by Rogers:

> Counseling consists of a definitely structured relationship highly permissive in nature, in which the client finds an opportunity to explore, freely and without defensiveness, his difficulties and emotionalized attitudes which sometimes surround them. As a result of this catharsis the client gains an understanding of himself which brings his behavior within the sphere of his own conscious control, and enables him to take positive steps in new directions in the light of his new orientation.[189]

Snyder, a student of Rogers and a spokesman for the school, has attempted to qualify this definition of counseling by the use of the adjective "psychotherapeutic" which effects a further specification of its nature. He defines psychotherapeutic counseling thus:

> ... a face-to-face relationship in which a psychologically trained individual is consciously attempting by verbal means to assist another person or persons to modify emotional attitudes that are socially maladjusted, and in which the sub-

[186]Rogers, *Counseling and Psychotherapy*, p. 3.
[187]Carl R. Rogers, "Counseling," *Review of Educational Research*, XV (1945), 155-63.
[188]*Ibid., Counseling and Psychotherapy*, p. 18.
[189]*Ibid., Review of Educational Research*, p. 155.

ject is relatively aware of the personality reorganization through which he is going.[190]

Rogers pointed out certain basic aspects of the counseling relationship which clarify its nature. First, the atmosphere is characterized by warmth and responsiveness[191] arising from the efforts of the counselor to create an affectional bond marked by warmth, interest, responsiveness, but with a definitely limited degree of emotional attachment.[192] Therapy is not merely being "nice" to a person in trouble. It is helping him to gain an insight into himself, to adjust to human relationships in a healthy fashion.[193]

Secondly, it is permissive in regard to the expression of feelings. All feelings and attitudes, no matter how guilty or shameful, may be expressed with the counselor accepting all statements without any moralistic or judgmental attitude.[194]

Certain therapeutic limits are a third important basic aspect of the counseling relationship, which help to structure the situation so that the client can make better use of it.[195] Time limits are set as an arbitrary human limit to which the client must adjust and they are maintained with a warm understanding of his need to break them.[196] The actions of the client are limited to the expression of feelings but not to harm others or their property by carrying all impulses into action.[197] This applies only to play therapy.[198]

The fourth characteristic is the freedom from any type of pressure or coercion. The hour is the client's hour, not the counselor's. Advice, suggestion, pressure to follow one course of action rather than another are out of place.[199] Thus positive ground is provided for growth and development, for conscious choice, and for self-directed integration.[200]

In this therapeutic relationship the client can be genuinely himself. He can evaluate his impulses, actions, conflicts, choices,

---

[190] William U. Snyder, "Present Status of Psychotherapeutic Counseling," *Psychological Bulletin*, XLIV (1947), 297-396.
[191] Rogers, *Counseling and Psychotherapy*, p. 87.
[192] *Ibid.*, p. 88.
[193] *Ibid.*, p. 105.
[194] *Ibid.*, p. 88.
[195] *Ibid.*, p. 89.
[196] *Ibid.*, p. 101.
[197] *Ibid.*, p. 89.
[198] *Ibid.*, p. 104.
[199] *Ibid.*, p. 89.
[200] *Ibid.*, p. 90.

past patterns and present problems, much more truly because he is freed from the necessity of self-defense and is protected from too complacent dependence.[201]

The counseling relationship is structured or defined by what the counselor does not do, i.e., make moral judgments or exert any pressure on the client,[202] as well as by the explanation of the counseling situation which he may offer, leaving the responsibility with the client,[203] yet making it clear that it is a joint enterprise providing the client with a way of proceeding to the solution of his problem.[204] Experience in therapy has inclined the client-centered therapist to "give up any attempt at 'structuring' though earlier these were thought to be of value."[205] Intellectual descriptions of the relationship of the counselor and client, or of the process, have proved to be of no help and sometimes a hindrance to therapy.[206]

Rogers explained the nature and effect of the counseling relationship in this way:

> The counseling relationship is one in which warmth of acceptance and absence of any coercion or personal pressure on the part of the counselor permits the maximum expression of feelings, attitudes, and problems by the counselee. The relationship is a well structured one, with limits of time, dependence, and of aggressive action which apply particularly to the client, and limits of responsibility and affection which the counselor imposes on himself. In this unique experience of complete emotional freedom within a well-defined framework, the client is free to recognize and understand his impulses and patterns, positive and negative, as in no other relationship.[207]

Rogers originally maintained that his counseling approach applied to the overwhelming majority of clients who have the capacity to achieve reasonably adequate solutions for their problems.[208] In general these are individuals of at least dull normal intelligence, emotionally free from family, sufficiently mature without too much rigidity of personality, free from ex-

---

[201] Ibid.
[202] Ibid., p. 91.
[203] Ibid., p. 96.
[204] Ibid., p. 93.
[205] Ibid., Client-Centered Therapy, p. 69.
[206] Ibid., p. 69.
[207] Ibid., Counseling and Psychotehrapy, p. 113.
[208] Ibid., p. 128.

cessive environmental limitations, and in most cases possessing a desire for help.[209]

Rogers now maintains that his tentative criteria for applicability have proved "less than helpful" because they have tended to engender an "evaluative, diagnostic frame of mind which has not been profitable" in the counselor.[210] He now believes there where a client-centered approach is consistently used it may be applicable to all people, though not as a cure for all psychological problems. He thus explains his position:

> An atmosphere of acceptance and respect, of deep understanding, is a good climate for personal growth, and as such applies to our children, our colleagues, our students, as well as to our clients, whether these be "normal," neurotic, or psychotic. This does *not* mean that it will *cure* every psychological condition. . . . Yet as a psychological climate which the individual can use for deeper self-understanding, for a reorganization of self in the direction of more realistic integration, for the development of more comfortable and mature ways of behaving — this is not an opportunity which is of use for some groups and not for others. It would appear rather to be a point of view which might in basic ways be applicable to all individuals, even though it might not resolve all problems or provide all the help which a particular individual needs.[211]

In discussing the ultimate aim of counseling, it was Rogers' opinion, that the newer approach to counseling differs from the others in that it has a genuinely different goal. The aim is not to solve a particular problem, but to assist the individual to *grow,* become more independent and integrated, so that he can cope with all problems in a better-integrated fashion.[212] He later modified this opinion about the ultimate goal of counseling in the following statement:

> Although the ultimate goal is somewhat similar — to establish the client as an independent and responsible person — the route by which this is reached is, on the one hand, tact-

---

[209]William U. Snyder, "Client-Centered Therapy," chap. xix. *An Introduction to Clinical Psychology* (New York: Roland Press, ed., Pennington and Berg, 1948), 473.

[210]Rogers, *Client-Centered Therapy,* p. 228.

[211]*Ibid.,* p. 230.

[212]*Ibid., Counseling and Psychotherapy,* p. 28.

ful guidance and direction, and on the other hand, release of the individual's strength and capacity.[213]
The therapeutic counseling of Rogers aims to aid the client in attaining a unified purpose of life, the courage or basic self-confidence to meet life and the obstacles which it presents in a constructive, satisfying way.[214] The counseling process is ordered to help the individual become a better-organized person, orientated around healthy goals, which he has seen clearly and definitely chosen.[215] Rogers expresses the ultimate goal of counseling in this way: "This reorientation and reorganization of self . . . is certainly the major aim and goal of counseling."[216]

The attainment of this ultimate aim is fostered through the execution of the proximate aim of the counseling experience. For Rogers this seems to consist in the promotion of catharsis leading to insight and choice.[217] He refers to this process as "one of the significant goals" of any counseling experience, which consists in bringing into the open thoughts, attitudes, feelings, and emotionally charged impulses centering around the problems and conflicts of the individual.[218] He orientates his theory and practice of counseling around this concept, and expresses the proximate aim in terms of counselor activity thus: "In effective counseling and psychotherapy one of the major purposes of the counselor is to help the client to express freely the emotionalized attitudes which are basic to his adjustment problems and conflicts."[219]

As implied in the consideration of the nature and aims of counseling above, Rogers makes several basic assumptions which should be specified before turning to the consideration of the methods or techniques which he proposes. One of these is that problems of adjustment are rarely of an intellectual nature alone, and if so can be solved in the realm of the intellect without counseling. He maintains the client's unrecognized emotionalized attitudes are usually basic, and it is with these that counseling

[213] Carl R. Rogers, "Psychotherapy," *Current Trends in Psychology* (Pittsburgh: University Press, 1947), p. 112.
[214] *Ibid., Counseling and Psychotherapy*, p. 218.
[215] *Ibid.*, p. 227.
[216] *Ibid.*, p. 194.
[217] *Ibid.*, p. 35.
[218] *Ibid.*, p. 131.
[219] *Ibid.*, p. 173.

is concerned.[220] A second basic assumption, regarded as a discovery, is that in most, if not all individuals there are forces of growth and tendencies toward positive self-initiated action that can be relied upon to attain the goals of counseling if a suitable psychological atmosphere is provided. Of these he states:

> The individual is capable of discovering and perceiving, truly and spontaneously, the interrelationships between his own attitudes, and the relationship of himself to reality. The individual has the capacity and the strength to devise, quite unguided, the steps which will lead him to a more mature and more comfortable relationship to his reality.[221]

Consistent counselor recognition that the individual has sufficient capacity to deal constructively with all aspects of his life which can potentially come into his conscious awareness, seems to be the optimal attitude for the client-centered counselor. As Rogers states, "This means the creation of an inter-personal situation in which material may come into the client's awareness, and a meaningful demonstration of the counselor's acceptance of the client as a person who is competent to direct himself."[222]

Turning to the methods of counseling Rogers now points out that the methods and techniques of client-centered therapy must be an implementation of "a coherent and developing set of attitudes deeply imbedded in" the personal organization of the counselor. Attitude of the counselor toward the client's capacity for growth is always basic to the use of technique and methods. As he notes,

> In our experience, the counselor who tries to use a "method" is doomed to be unsuccessful unless this method is genuinely in line with his own attitudes. On the other hand, the counselor whose attitudes are of the type which facilitate therapy may be only partially successful, because his attitudes are inadequately implemented by appropriate methods and techniques.[223]

---

[220]Ibid., p. 131.
[221]Carl R. Rogers, "Significant Aspects of Client-Centered Therapy," American Psychologist, I (1946), 418.
[222]Ibid., Client-Centered Therapy, p. 24.
[223]Ibid., pp. 19, 20.

The surest route to the important issues, the painful conflicts, to the areas with which counseling may deal is to follow the client's pattern of feelings as it is expressed.[224] The best techniques for interviewing are those which encourage the free expression of feeling, with the counselor consciously refraining from any activity or response which would guide the direction of the interview or the content brought forth.[225] Negatively, as Rogers now recognizes,[226] this means that the counselor refrains from questioning, probing, blaming, interpreting, advising, suggesting, persuading, or reassuring, though some of these practices were allowed in earlier works. Positively, it means that the counselor uses only those techniques in the interview which convey his deep understanding of the emotionalized attitudes expressed, and his acceptance of them with neither approval nor disapproval. It was formerly proposed that this be accomplished by a sensitive reflection and clarification of the client's attitudes.[227] Now, as Rogers notes, "we have tended to give up the description of the counselor's role as being that of clarifying the client's attitudes."[228] Rogers explains the modification of his theory in this way:

> At the present stage of thinking in client-centered therapy there is another attempt to describe . . . the way in which the basic hypothesis is implemented. This formulation would state that it is the counselor's function to assume, in so far as he is able, the internal frame of reference of the client, to perceive the world as the client sees it, to perceive the client himself as he is seen by himself, to lay aside all perceptions from the external frame of reference while doing so, and to communicate something of this emphatic understanding to the client.[229]

It was formerly maintained that the counselor's skillful use of the major technique[230] of recognizing and accepting, clarifying and reflecting of the client's emotionalized attitudes initi-

---

[224]Ibid., *Counseling and Psychotherapy*, p. 131.
[225]Ibid.
[226]Ibid., *Client-Centered Therapy*, p. 31.
[227]Ibid., *Counseling and Psychotherapy*, p. 173.
[228]Ibid., *Client-Centered Therapy*, p. 28.
[229]Ibid., p. 29.
[230]Ibid., *Review of Educational Research*, p. 155.

ated and promoted three phases of counseling to the attainment of both the proximate and the ultimate goals of the process.[231] It now appears that the same process is instituted by the counselor's concentrated effort to convey an emphatic understanding of the client's attitudes and feelings.[222]

The initial phase of catharsis involving gradual emotional release from repressed feelings through the expression and recognition of emotionalized attitudes leads from superficial to deeper problems and attitudes that have been denied to consciousness.[233] Catharsis inevitably leads to insight which develops for the most part spontaneously..[234]

In the insight phase, involving a more adequate facing of reality, the relating of problems to each other, the perception of patterns of behavior, the acceptance of denied elements of self and the making of new plans, the primary technique of the counselor remains the same.[235] The counselor concentrates his whole effort upon achieving a deep understanding of the private world of the client.[236] As Rogers points out,

> The counselor says in effect, "To be of assistance to you I will put aside myself — the self of ordinary interaction — and enter into your world of perception as completely as I am able. I will become, in a sense, another self for you — an alter ego of your own attitudes and feelings — a safe opportunity for you to discern yourself more clearly, to experience yourself more truly and deeply, to choose more significantly."[237]

The resulting third phase is marked by the increase in positive choice of new ways of behaving in conformity with the newly organized concept of self,[238] and self-initiated actions which are most significant for growth, even though they relate only to minor issues. These actions tend to create new confidence and independence in the client, reinforcing his new orientation through increased insight.[239] Later steps of the client

[231] Ibid., *American Psychologist*, p. 417.
[232] Ibid., *Client-Centered Therapy*, p. 29.
[233] Ibid., *American Psychologist*, p. 417.
[234] Ibid., *Counseling and Psychotherapy*, p. 216.
[235] Ibid., *American Psychologist*, p. 417.
[236] Ibid., *Client-Centered Therapy*, p. 30.
[237] Ibid., p. 35.
[238] Ibid., *American Psychologist*, p. 417.
[239] Ibid., *Counseling and Psychotherapy*, p. 216.

implement more and more completely the new concept of self, and this process once begun continues beyond the counseling interviews in the direction of greater psychological growth and maturity. The client's new behavior will be more spontaneous and less tense, more in harmony with the social needs of others, and will represent a more realistic and comfortable adjustment to life.[240]

In Rogers' theory of counseling there is no distinct method of re-education. The counselor makes no attempt to solve the client's problems through re-education or retraining the individual in all aspects of life. For Rogers re-education is confined to giving the client sufficient practice in the application of new insights to build up his confidence and enable him to proceed in a healthy fashion without the support of the counseling relationship.[241] "These re-educative experiences are, for the most part, the achievement of an expanding insight and the multiplication of positive steps already initiated."[242]

If in the course of the process the client seems actually to lack necessary information and expresses a need for it, the counselor is likely to refer him to a convenient source. He avoids giving it himself because to do so has been found to alter the counselor-client relationship, placing the responsibility for the progress of counseling on the counselor, rather than maintaining it as a joint responsibility.[243]

For similar reasons the counselor avoids environmental manipulations such as using his influence with officials on behalf of the client. These are considered to be beyond the range of the counseling relationship.[244]

Psychometric tests are almost never used on the initiative of the counselor because of Rogers' belief that the use of such tests can interfere with the process of therapy.[245] Rogers sug-

[240]*Ibid., American Psychologists*, p. 417.
[241]*Ibid., Counseling and Psychotherapy*, p. 218.
[242]*Ibid.*
[243]Snyder, "Client-Centered Therapy," *An Introduction to Clinical Psychology*, p. 467.
[244]*Ibid.*, p. 469.
[245]Carl R. Rogers, "Psychometric Tests in Client-Centered Counseling," *Educational and Psychological Measurements*, VI (1946), 139-44.

gests that the counselor should lay aside all diagnostic attitudes toward the client in favor of the client-centered nature of the therapeutic relationship.

The therapist must lay aside his preoccupation with diagnosis and his diagnostic shrewdness, must discard his tendency to make professional evaluations, must cease his endeavors to formulate an accurate prognosis, must give up the temptation subtly to guide the individual, and must concentrate on one purpose only: that of providing deep understanding and acceptance of the attitudes consciously held at the moment by the client as he explores step by step into the dangerous areas which he has been denying to consciousness.[246]

In his most recent book, Rogers explains that "self-diagnosis" by the client replaces the professional diagnosis by the counselor.

In client-centered therapy the purpose of the therapist is to provide the conditions in which the client is able to make, to experience, and accept the diagnosis of the psychogenic aspects of his maladjustment.[247]

Rogers originally enumerated twelve steps that are characteristic of the therapeutic process of counseling. These would, perhaps, be modified somewhat in view of the modifications in his general theory and practice. The original steps can be summarized as follows:

1. The individual comes for help. Rightly recognized this is one of the most important steps in therapy. The individual has taken himself in hand and taken responsible action of the first importance. If the client accepts responsibility for bringing himself, he also accepts responsibility for working on his problem.[248, 249]

2. The helping situation is usually defined. The counselor does not have the answers, but the counseling situation does provide a place where the client can, with assistance, work out his own solutions to his problems. The client is helped to feel that the counseling hour is his to use, to take responsibility for, an opportunity freely to be himself.[250, 251]

[246]*Ibid., American Psychologist*, p. 421.
[247]*Ibid., Client-Centered Therapy*, p. 223.
[248]*Ibid., Counseling and Psychotherapy*, p. 31.
[249]*Ibid.*, p. 32.
[250]*Ibid.*, p. 33.
[251]*Ibid.*, p. 35.

3. The counselor encourages free expression of feelings. This is brought about by the counselor's friendly, interested, receptive attitude, and the skill in using the techniques of catharsis.[252]

4. The counselor accepts, recognizes, and clarifies negative feelings expressed by the client without approval or blame.[253]

5. Client expresses faint and tentative impulses which make for growth.[254]

6. Counselor accepts and recognizes the expressed positive feelings without approval or praise.[255]

7. Client insight, understanding, and acceptance of self begin to come spontaneously.[256]

8. Intermingled with the insight process is a process of clarification of possible decisions and courses of action.[257]

9. Client initiates minute, but highly significant, positive actions.[258]

10. Development of further insight and more complete and accurate self-understanding as the individual gains courage to see more deeply into his own actions.[259]

11. Client takes increasingly integrated positive actions, has less fear about making choices and more confidence in self-directed action.[260]

12. There is a feeling of decreasing need for help, and recognition on the part of the client that the relationship must end.[261]

In *Client-Centered Therapy* Rogers has included a chapter which contains a generalized statement of personality dynamics and behavior to explain the research evidence which has been gathered. He presents his theory in the form of nineteen propositions under the title of "A Theory of Personality and Behavior."[262] Rogers thus summarizes his theory in its most general aspects:

> This chapter has endeavored to present a theory of personality and behavior which is consistent with our experience and research in client-centered therapy. The theory is basically phenomenological in character, and relies heavily upon the concept of the self as an explanatory construct.

[252]*Ibid.*
[253]*Ibid.*, p. 37.
[254]*Ibid.*, p. 39.
[255]*Ibid.*, p. 40.
[256]*Ibid.*
[257]*Ibid.*, p. 41.
[258]*Ibid.*
[259]*Ibid.*, p. 43.
[260]*Ibid.*
[261]*Ibid.*, p. 44.
[262]*Ibid.*, *Client-Centered Therapy*, pp. 481-533.

It pictures the end-point of personality development as being a basic congruence between the phenomenal field of experience and the conceptual structure of the self — a situation which, if achieved, would represent freedom from internal strain and anxiety, and freedom from potential strain; which would represent the maximum in realistically orientated adaption; which would mean the establishment of an individualized value system having considerable identity with the value system of any other equally well-adjusted member of the human race.[263]

It is Rogers' hope that the hypotheses of his theory will stimulate significant study of the deeper dynamics of human behavior.

---

[263]*Ibid.*, p. 532.

CHAPTER III

COMPARISON AND IMPLICATIONS OF CURRENT THEORIES

Agreements and Differences

In the first chapter of this study the opinion of Arbuckle was cited that regardless of other differences most clinical counselors agree that counseling is a "person-to-person" relationship and that "its basic concern is human development."[1] This opinion seems to be verified by the five representatives whose theories have been presented in the previous chapter.

General points of agreement. — Jones considers counseling as "a personal and dynamic relationship between two individuals."[2] Strang presents her notion as "a face-to-face relationship."[3] Williamson describes counseling as "a one-to-one relationship in learning."[4] Mathewson insists that the first fundamental character of counseling is "direct personal communication between counselor and client."[5] Rogers seems to concur when he presents counseling as "the face-to-face situation" and as a "therapeutic relationship" between counselor and client.[6] Although Rogers maintains that this relationship can be extended to small group situations,[7] it seems that there is essential agreement among these five representatives that the basic element in counseling is the presence of at least two human beings in the act of personal communication.

Another commonly accepted element in counseling seems to be the mutual consideration of a problem, difficulty, or maladjustment which is proper to one of the individuals, and provides

[1] Arbuckle, *Teacher Counseling*, p. 5.
[2] Jones, *Principles of Guidance*, p. 269.
[3] Strang, *Counseling Technics in College and Secondary Schools*, p. 11.
[4] Williamson, *Counseling Adolescents*, p. 4.
[5] Mathewson, *Guidance Policy and Practice*, p. 194.
[6] Rogers, "Counseling," *Review of Educational Research*, XV, 155.
[7] *Ibid.*, *American Psychologist*, I, 416.

part of the reason for the present relationship. In this Jones,[8] Strang,[9] Williamson,[10] Mathewson,[11] and Rogers,[12] would readily agree.

A second reason for the relationship seems to be the expression or implication of some sort of superiority in the individual who fills the role of counselor. This superiority may be in age or maturity, experience, knowledge, wisdom, or in skill. The five authorities concerned in this study would agree to the fact of counselor superiority though there seems to be a real difference of opinion among them as to the nature of this superiority.

Jones explicitly states in his definition of counseling that the counselor is either older, or more experienced, or wiser than the client, and he implies that the counselor should have a superiority of skill. It is because of this superiority that the counselor is able to be of some help to the client in his present difficulties.[13]

Strang seems to imply the counselor superiority in skill, experience, knowledge, and wisdom when she allows the counselor to supply information and make environmental changes.[14] to help the client "gain insight, new orientation, a more acceptable self-concept, better ways of thinking about problems and relationships, and new technics of living."[15]

Williamson implies maturity as well as skill, experience, knowledge, and wisdom in the counselor when he describes counseling as a "fundamental technique,[16] "a methodology"[17] of assisting an individual to achieve both immediate personal adustment and prepare for remote adult adustment through "a one-to-one relationship in learning."[18]

[8]Jones, *Principles of Guidance*, p. 269.
[9]Strang, *Counseling Technics*, p. 15.
[10]Williamson, *Counseling Adolescents*, p. 209.
[11]Mathewson, *Guidance Policy and Practice*, p. 208.
[12]Rogers, *Counseling and Psychotherapy*, p. 18.
[13]Jones, *Principles of Guidance*, p. 268.
[14]Strang, *Counseling Technics*, p. 11.
[15]*Ibid.*, p. 7.
[16]Williamson, *Counseling Adolescents*, p. 3.
[17]*Ibid.*, p. 110.
[18]*Ibid.*, p. 4.

Similarly, Mathewson seems to imply counselor superiority in maturity, knowledge, wisdom, experience, and skill when he formulates the role of the counselor as that of a "professional and personal socio-psychological interpreter," who cooperates with the client "in mutual review and analysis of the problem situation."[19]

For Rogers the superiority of the counselor would not of necessity be in knowledge, wisdom, experience, or maturity but would consist of a superiority of skill. It is his contention that "certain basic skills and attitudes" of the counselor can create "a psychological atmosphere which releases, frees, and utilizes deep strengths"[20] in the client which will enable the client "to devise, quite unguided, the steps which will lead him to a more mature and more comfortable relationship with his reality."[21]

In the light of these considerations it seems to be true that there is a substantial agreement and acceptance of the most general characteristics of counseling. The representative authorities in this study would all accept the personal nature of counseling, the mutual concern for problems, difficulties, and maladjustments, and the fact of counselor superiority. However, the differences of opinion concerning the nature of the counselor superiority would seem to indicate a basically different conception of the nature of counseling itself.

The authorities of the traditional school, for the most part, think of counseling as an educational process, with the counselor acting in the role of a professional teacher. In this context it is to be noted that Jones considers counseling "a distinctly educational process" which resembles somewhat the "manner used by Socrates."[22] For Williamson counseling is a "life adustment type of teacher-student learning experience."[23] Mathewson's position is clear from the following statement:

> For the client, counselor, and institutions . . . the dominating conception in counseling must be an educational

[19] Mathewson, *Guidance Policy and Practice*, p. 207.
[20] Rogers, *American Psychologist*, I, 422.
[21] *Ibid.*, p. 418.
[22] Jones, *Principles of Guidance*, p. 269.
[23] Williamson, *Counseling Adolescents*, p. 110.

one: the attainment of an educational aim by educative means.[24]

Strang is not as definitive or explicit but her conception of counseling and the role of the counselor and the client in the process has a decidedly teacher-student implication. She states:

> Counseling at its best is the art by which a person is helped to understand himself, his relations to others, and the world in which he lives. It is a learning experience for the student.[25]

This view of Strang, coupled with her insistence that "the counselor may facilitate the process by supplying information,"[26] seems sufficient to indicate her agreement with the other members of the traditional school.

For this group, counseling is essentially an educational process. It is a process of learning for the student and a kind of personal teaching for the counselor. The learning and the teaching are not too different from the same process as they function in the tutorial system. There is, however, one important difference. The subject matter to be learned is not always a well defined body of knowledge that is more or less exact and certain, but the contingent and variable elements of human adjustment and growth in self-directive abilities.

It is presupposed by the traditional school that the counselor can be of service to the client in solving his difficulties or in overcoming his maladjustments because the former possess some qualities or abilities which the latter lacks. These qualities or abilities may be any or all of the following: more mature attitudes or habits, experimental or theoretical knowledge and wisdom, or simply, skill in the arts of self-direction. It is further supposed that the counselor is able to communicate to the client, or otherwise help him to acquire some of these qualities or abilities through the counseling relationship, which remains essentially a student-teacher relationship.

Although Rogers agrees with the traditionalists in regard to the most general characteristics of counseling as noted above, he does not conceive of the process or the relationship between

---

[24]Mathewson, *Guidance Policy and Practice*, p. 207.
[25]Strang, *Counseling Technics*, p. 15.
[26]*Ibid.*, p. 11.

counselor and client as an educational one. In his theory the counselor is never a teacher. Nor is the client cast in the role of a student, at least not as a student who is to be taught in the generally accepted meaning of the term. This does not mean that learning is not needed for readjustment or that it is not to be fostered through the counseling process. It simply means that Rogers would promote the learning, growth, and development of the client by means other than teaching.

Rogers presents counseling as a therapeutic or curative process. The relationship between the counselor and the client is a therapeutic relationship. This means that the task of the counselor is not to teach, but to create a psychological atmosphere characterized by warmth and responsiveness,[27] permissiveness[28] and freedom from pressure[29] in which the client may learn through discovery what he needs to learn for solving his problems or overcoming his maladjustments. The client can acocmplish this learning by discovery because through the counseling relationship and atmosphere he is provided with "positive ground for growth and development, for conscious choice, and for self-directed integration.[30]

In the light of these facts the differences in the two concepts of counseling seem to be founded on two aspects of the learning process. On the one hand the traditional counselors maintain that some of the learning and development which is necessary to help the client solve his difficulties can be attained by teaching within a teacher-student relationship.

Rogers, on the other hand, insists that the necessary learning and development cannot be effectively promoted by teaching or within a teacher-student relationship, but can be effectively fostered by skillfully assisting the client's powers of discovery — a position that follows from the fundamental assumption that present difficulties of the client have arisen not from a lack of intellectual learning, whether speculative or practical, but rather from unrecognized emotional attitudes which render

[27] Rogers, *Counseling and Psychotherapy*, p. 87.
[28] *Ibid.*, p. 88.
[29] *Ibid.*, p. 89.
[30] *Ibid.*, p. 30.

that learning or any new learning ineffective.[31] Through the therapeutic counseling process the client can be assisted both to more effective use of his learning, and to the attainment of new learning for the solution of his problems and readjustments. This insight-learning will be discovered by the client "for the most part spontaneously" within the therapeutic counseling setting.[32]

Consideration of the aims of counseling helps to clarify these differences of opinion concerning the nature of counseling. In the analysis of the previous chapter a distinction was indicated between the ultimate and the proximate aim of the process. This distinction is made to specify and order the expressed purposes of counseling. The ultimate aim represents the overall good of the client to be sought through counseling. It is the chief reason for the beginning of the process. The immediate purpose or aim of the counselor as he approaches the counseling relationship is called the proximate aim. In another order this subordinate aim might be referred to as a means to the ultimate goal of counseling.

The authorities examined in this study differ somewhat in expression, but seem to be in general though limited agreement as to the ultimate aim of counseling. They are individually concerned with assisting clients to achieve optimum personal development of their potentialities[33] within the limits of both personal and social satisfaction,[34] to develop their ability wisely to solve their own problems unassisted,[35] to achieve optimum self-realization for social purposes,[36] to attain the highest possible self-realization consistent with social obligations and moral values,[37] and to help the clients become better organized persons, orientated around healthy goals, which they have clearly seen and definitely chosen.[38]

[31] *Ibid.*, p. 131.
[32] *Ibid.*, p. 216.
[33] Williamson, *Counseling Adolescents*, p. 27.
[34] *Ibid.*, p. 222.
[35] Jones, *Principles of Guidance*, p. 270.
[36] Strang, *Counseling Technics*, p. 15.
[37] Mathewson, *Guidance Policy and Practice*, p. 207.
[38] Rogers, *Counseling and Psychotherapy*, p. 227.

All of these expressions of the ultimate aim of counseling seem to point toward helping the client obtain the fullest possible personal development in accordance with some standard, which implies his independence and integration or the ability to handle himself and his problems both present and future in a more mature manner.

The unanimity of the authorities is not complete. It is to be noted that there does seem to be a real difference among them in respect to the standard which measures or regulates the development of the client. For the traditional counselors this standard is an objective one consisting of conformity to social or moral values. For Rogers this standard seems to be subjective, and may or may not coincide with objective values, either social or moral. In his theory this consideration seems to be beyond the concern of the counselor. The criterion for the "healthy goals" that Rogers speaks of is not objectivity but rather the psychological comfort of the client in relation to his reality.[39] Concern for objectivity is sacrificed in favor of what is proposed as a more direct approach toward the client's greater psychological independence and integrity.[40] It is here in respect to the standard of client development that another fundamental difference between the traditional and the client-centered theory of counseling is found. This fact becomes more evident with the consideration of the proximate aim of counseling.

Jones, who thinks of counseling as a means of giving direct assistance to the client in reference to his problems,[41] presents the proximate aim of counseling as the clearer definition of the problems or difficulties.[42] To this end he proposes open discussion, the gathering and analysis of all the facts, and the focusing of experience upon them.

Strang, following her "social" standard and teacher-student concept of counseling, would have the counselor aim at helping the client understand what he "can and should do" to strengthen his best qualities, handle his difficulties in a rational way, find suitable channels for his emotions, and move toward his "more

[39]Rogers, *American Psychologist*, I, 418.
[40]*Ibid.*, *Counseling and Psychotherapy*, p. 28.
[41]Jones, *Principles of Guidance*, p. 80.
[42]*Ibid.*, p. 269.

accceptable self," which implies a concern for the welfare of all.[43]

Williamson logically proposes that the counselor aim to aid the "client in learning the ways and means to continue growth"[44] and optimum development that is both "personally satisfying and socially satisfactory."[45] For him this aid seems to consist primarily in helping the client understand the relationship of analysis, diagnosis, prognosis, and counseling to the solution of difficulties and as the "initial steps in a life time sequence" of adjustment and readjustment.[46] The counselor's aim is not only to provide therapy, insight, confirmation of choices, and information but also to help the client acquire a "basic understanding and skill in using" these methods.[47]

Mathewson proposes that the counselor stimulate the client's powers of learning, adjustability, development, and integration "on the level of conscious apprehension and evaluative reasoning"[48] by giving aid of an "educative, psychological nature,"[49] in view of social obligations and moral values. This may have to do with the understanding of the situation, or of himself and his behavior, learning about pertinent factors in the environmental situation, definite plans of action, or specific ways of developing personal capabilities to become more "effectively purposive and self-directive."[50]

In the therapeutic counseling proposed by Rogers the counselor is not interested in "doing something *to* the individual," or of "inducing him to do something about himself."[51] The counselor is not a teacher trying to motivate, increase understanding, clarify issues, or impart skills by teaching methods, but a therapist who is attempting to free the client for normal growth and development by "removing obstacles so that he can again move

[43] Strang, *Counseling Technics*, p. 15.
[44] Williamson, *Counseling Adolescents*, p. 24.
[45] *Ibid.*, p. 222.
[46] *Ibid.*, p. 213.
[47] *Ibid.*, p. 215.
[48] Mathewson, *Guidance Policy and Practice*, p. 207.
[49] Mathewson, *Harvard Educational Review*, XVII, 22.
[50] *Ibid.*, *Guidance Policy and Practice*, p. 207.
[51] Rogers, *Counseling and Psychotherapy*, p. 29.

forward."[52] Consequently, one of the major purposes of the counselor is to help the client express, recognize, and accept the emotional thoughts, attitudes, and impulses that are basic to his adjustment problems and conflicts."[53] This is to promote catharsis which will lead to spontaneous insight and choice,[54] acceptance of self and values and thus to better personal organization and "more comfortable relationship to his reality."[55]

The differences of opinion among the authorities regarding the proximate aim of counseling seem to be obvious. As they differ in this respect they naturally become more diverse in the proposal of particular methods to reach their goal.

Among the traditional counselors there seems to be general agreement that the counselor must prepare for the counseling interview by careful analysis and review of all available data on the client.[56] This includes the analysis and synthesis of information gathered from observation, testing, daily schedules, and physical examination.[57] Diagnosis in cooperation with the client follows, and involves problem identification, search for its cause, and indication of steps to satisfactory adjustment.[58] This procedure is defined as the art of evaluation, interpretation, and prognostic significance of data.[59] It seems to be necessary as a part of counseling to bring into full view of both counselor and client the factors that can be correlated, thought about, and deliberately acted upon.[60] In this theory interviewing, appraisal, and evaluation activities are closely interrelated and are seen as a unified and interlocking action with varying participation of the counselor and the client according to the nature of the problem situation and the needs of the client.[61]

In the theory of Rogers the gathering, review, and analysis of information about the client is considered superfluous and

[52]*Ibid.*
[53]*Ibid.*, p. 172.
[54]*Ibid.*, p. 35.
[55]Rogers, *American Psychologist*, I, 418.
[56]Jones, *Principles of Guidance*, p. 274.
[57]Strang, *Counseling Technics*, p. 19.
[58]Williamson, *Counseling Adolescents*, p. 185.
[59]*Ibid.*, p. 207.
[60]Mathewson, *Guidance Policy and Practice*, p. 196.
[61]*Ibid.*, p. 197.

even harmful to the process of therapy. It tends to prejudice the counselor and impose undue responsibility upon him. Tests are almost never used to gather information about the client unless the client himself requests them or in rare cases to determine the fitness of the client for this type of therapy. It is maintained that the client will introduce any information that is of importance to him in the solution of his problems and difficulties. In the interest of the therapeutic relationship the counselor must not diagnose, make professional evaluations, nor attempt to formulate prognosis. He must not in any way attempt to guide subtly the individual as he explores the areas of his problems that he has been denying to consciousness. The counselor does not attend to the intellectual content verbalized by the client, but must concentrate on "one purpose only," that of providing deep understanding and acceptance of the situation expressed by the client at the moment.[62]

Following these differences there are diverse recommendations for the counseling interview itself. According to Jones, and others of the traditional school the counseling interview is conducted in an atmosphere of friendliness and mutual confidence with the counselor avoiding critical and condemnatory attitudes and attempting to accept as well as understand the client as he is. The counselor keeps control of the interview but guides it unobtrusively as he helps the client come to grips with his problem, do his own thinking, reach his own conclusions, and change his own feelings and behavior. The counselor tries to see that the client's thinking is challenged, and that he has the needed facts and insight to make sound judgments. The counselor helps to draw up a reasonable plan of action for the immediate and the remote future before the end of the interview.[63]

Strang notes the importance of securing the client's cooperation and his assumption of responsibility to use the resources available to him in the counseling relationship. She proposes that the counselor listen, accept, and reflect the client's feelings, and make interpretations according to the needs of the

[62]Rogers, *American Psychologist*, I, 421.
[63]Jones, *Principles of Guidance*, pp. 274-76.

client. In general she recommends the use of any technique that will help the client clarify his feelings and lead him to genuine insight. She proposes that the counselor offer positive help in putting these insights to work in suitable educational opportunities, jobs, and recreational groups. Continuation of therapy outside the interview is to be encouraged to attain the maximum growth.[64]

Williamson adds that there are no standard techniques in either diagnosing or counseling and in his opinion the effective counselor is the one who adapts his techniques of advising to the personality of the client. He recommends that as the counselor should be prepared to help the client solve, master, choose, learn, and deal with a wide variety of situations he must have a repertoire of specific techniques. In assisting the client to understand himself the counselor translates technical facts from the analysis, asks questions, watches the client reactions, and then directs the conversation accordingly. He begins advising at the point of the student's understanding, explaining why he advises what he does and the implications for the client's adjustment. Very often the counselor is able to assist the client in carrying out the plan of action that has been formulated.[65]

Mathewson seems to be in agreement with the other counselors of the traditional school. It is his opinion that to be effective in the appraisal phase of counseling the counselor must have knowledge of the "situational" scene, and he will have to convey specific information and make interpretations to assist the client obtain necessary insights. This will be true even when all the facts are possessed by the client. It is particularly in the evaluative phase that the professional skill and the technical knowledge of the counselor are required to assist the client in evaluating and correlating the pertinent case factors effectively, without undue imposition of his own personality.[66]

True to his suppositions Rogers recommends that the best techniques for interviewing are those that encourage free expression of feeling, with the counselor consciously refraining

[64]Strang, *Counseling Technics*, pp. 121-136.
[65]Williamson, *Counseling Adolescents*, pp 217-37.
[66]Mathewson, *Harvard Educational Review*, XVII, 20.

from any activity or response that would guide the direction of the interview or the content brought forth. The counselor may explain the counseling process to the client, though experience has tended to show that intellectual descriptions of the relationship of counselor and client or of the process are of little value. The counselor assumes no responsibility for the solution of problems, but emphasizes that the counseling situation does provide a place where the client can, with the help of the counselor, work out his own solution to his problem. The counselor encourages the free expression of feelings by word as well as by his friendly, interested, and receptive attitude and the skillful use of his technique. The counselor must carefully avoid questioning, probing, blaming, interpreting, advising, suggesting, persuading, or reassuring. He uses only those techniques that convey his deep understanding of the client as he sees himself. This is best accomplished by the skillful use of the major technique of recognizing, accepting, and conveying an emphatic understanding of the client's attitudes and feelings.

In this manner the three phases of counseling are instituted and brought to completion. The first phase is that of catharsis and involves the gradual release of repressed feelings. These the counselor accepts and verbally recognizes without approval or disapproval, whether they are negative or positive, ambivalent or contradictory. This technique is used until insightful understanding appears spontaneously. It is then that the second phase of the process begins in which client insight becomes the most significant element. The same technique is used to strengthen and foster deeper client insights. In the final or choice phase there is an increase in positive choices and independent actions by the client. Here also the primary technique is the same until the client manifests a feeling of decreasing need for help. At this time the counseling relationship must end as it has reached its proposed goal of psychological independence and integrity of the client. It is understood that the client may return when and if he wishes.

In summation there seem to be several general points of agreement between the traditional concept of counseling and the client-centered theory of Rogers. These may be briefly stated as follows:

1. Counseling is basically personal in nature involving two individuals in active face-to-face communication.

2. Counseling always implies the mutual concern of the counselor and the client for the client with his problems, difficulties, or maladjustments.

3. Counseling always implies some kind of superiority in the counselor which makes him apt to be of help to the client in his need.

4. Counseling aims to help the client obtain optimum personal development so that he can handle himself and his problems, both present and future, in a more mature manner.

The differences between these two theories seem to be more numerous and may be summarized in the order of this investigation as follows:

I. Differences in regard to the nature of counseling:
   A. Traditional counselors think of counseling as an educational process with the relationship of counselor and client remaining essentially a student-teacher relationship characterized by friendliness, mutual confidence, acceptance, and permissiveness through which the client may learn, by teaching or discovery, what is necessary for the solution of his problems and the acquisition of self-directive abilities.
   B. Rogers thinks of counseling as a therapeutic process with a therapeutic relationship between counselor and client characterized by warmth, responsiveness, permissiveness, and freedom from pressure in which the client is freed from emotional impediments to growth and development and in which he may, with understanding help of the counselor, discover the elements for his self-directed reorganization.

II. Difference in regard to the aims of counseling:
   A. Ultimate Aim:
      1. The traditional counselors maintain that the optimum development of the client in counseling is measured by conformity to social and moral values.
      2. Rogers maintains that in view of the psychological independence and integrity of the client the measure of the client development in counseling is his psychological comfort in relation to his reality. Adjustment will result in deeply socialized values.

B. Proximate Aim:
1. The traditional counselors advocate the clearer definition of the problems and difficulties, or helping the client understand what he can and should do to strengthen his best qualities, handle his difficulties in a rational way, find suitable channels for his emotions, move toward his more acceptable social self, or helping the client acquire a basic understanding and skill in using the methods of analysis, diagnosis, prognosis, and counseling, or stimulating the client's powers of learning, adjustability, development, and integration by giving aid of an educational nature in view of the social obligations and moral values.
2. Rogers proposes that the counselor should free the client for normal growth and development by removing the emotional obstacles which impede his progress. The major purpose of the counselor is to demonstrate understanding and acceptance and promote catharsis which will lead client to spontaneous insight, new choices, acceptance of self and of values, better personal organization, psychological independence, and integration.

III. Differences in methods:
A. General Methods:
1. Traditional counselors advocate the mutual gathering, diagnosis, interpretation, and evaluation of all the facts about the client and his situation so that all factors that can be correlated, thought about, and acted upon are in full view of both counselor and client. In this process the participation of the counselor and the client may vary according to the nature of the problem situation and the needs of the client.
2. Rogers finds the gathering of information about the client and his situation prejudicial to the process of therapy. Tests are not advised unless the client requests them. There is no professional diagnosis, evaluation, or attempt at accurate prognosis. Diagnosis is left in the hands of the client. The counselor makes no attempt to guide the client as he explores his problems but concentrates on providing deep

understanding and acceptance of the emotional attitudes expressed by the client at the moment.
B. Particular Methods:
1. The recommendations of the traditional counselors for the counseling interview are in brief:
   a) the atmosphere of the interview is marked by friendliness, mutual confidence, acceptance, understanding, permissiveness, avoidance of criticism and moralizing.
   b) there should be professional control of the interview and the cooperation of the client is secured by establishing rapport.
   c) the counselor should attempt to challenge the thinking of the client, and see that he has all the facts and insights to make sound judgments. In general the counselor uses any technique that will help the client. He listens, reflects, and clarifies emotions, makes interpretations, or gives information according to the need of the client.
2. Rogers' recommendations may be summarized thus:
   a) the counselor attempts to create an atmosphere characterized by warmth, acceptance, responsiveness, permissiveness, and freedom from pressure in which the client may grow and develop normally.
   b) the counselor structures the counseling relationship by what he does not do rather than by what he says. The client assumes the major responsibility to work on his own problems with the understanding help of the counselor, observing the limits of time and action, with the assurance that the counseling time is his to use as he will toward the solution of his difficulties.
   c) the counselor consciously avoids any activity or response that would guide the direction of the interview or the content that is brought forth by the client.
   d) the counselor encourages the client to express any feelings related to his difficulties and then uses only those techniques that convey his deep understanding and acceptance of these with neither approval or disapproval.

e) the purposes of counseling through the three phases of catharsis, insight, and choice are best attained by the skillful use of the major techniques of recognizing, understanding, accepting, and reflecting of the client's attitudes as they are expressed.

Philosophical and Psychological Implications

The agreement noted between the traditional counselors and Rogers in reference to the four basic aspects of counseling, though general in nature, seem sufficient to indicate the direction that this investigation must take to arrive at a valid philosophical and psychological evaluation of the proposals made by each school. These agreements not only serve as a point of contact between the two theories of counseling but they also function in the same capacity in relation to the scholastic synthesis from which the principles of evaluation are to be drawn in this study. The following observations will clarify this position.

The analysis and comparison that have been made indicate that the representatives of both schools of counseling conceive of the process as a specific means to be used in helping the client maximize his self-directive and self-regulatory powers. None of the authorities studied are content to think of counseling merely as a means to help the client solve his immediate difficulties and problems. The mutual concern of the counselor and the client for the present difficulties and maladjustments of the client, though basic in the process, is but an occasion for the institution of this special type of assistance ordered to a more ultimate goal. Beyond the rectification of the immediate problems it is desired that the counseling experience should prepare the client to meet future difficulties in a more mature manner. There is a certain expectation that a more or less permanent residuum or power of perfectibility in the client can be catalyzed, activated, and strengthened through the counseling process so that the present difficulties can be overcome and future difficulties handled in a more efficient and satisfactory manner. The help of the counselor, who is particularly fitted for his role in the process by some perfection of nature, education, or professional training, is considered necessary to assist the client in attaining those self-directive and self-regulatory abilities which are indicative of his increased maturity.

Beyond these general agreements all the other differences that have been noted in regard to the specific nature, aims, and methods of counseling arise and remain as a source of controversy between the two schools. For the purpose of this study it does not seem possible to reconcile these differences or even evaluate them objectively by the accumulation and citation of experimental evidence alone. While the latter is not to be neglected in determining the effectiveness of particular techniques of counseling, it cannot serve as an adequate basis for the adoption of the more universal proposals made by either group regarding the controverted issues. Another source must be consulted to provide the general principles of judgment and evaluation for the objective weighing of the postulates proper to each school.

As there seems to be general agreement among the cited authorities of both schools that the process of counseling is a practical operation ordered to the overall good of the client in the order of action, that is, to the more or less permanent development of the self-directive and self-regulatory abilities of the client, it is philosophically reasonable to seek the scholastic principles of evaluation and judgment for the total process in terms of this aim. The reasonableness of this position is based upon the understanding of the influence exercised by the end or goal in any practical endeavor. It is clear to the scholastic that the end, aim, or goal of any operation or activity is always the rule and measure of whatever is done to reach this goal. Thus due proportion and relationship to the end in view become inherent perfections of any action performed to reach this end. If it were otherwise the desired goal could never be reached, unless by chance.

The ultimate or controlling aim of the counseling process as proposed by the counseling authorities is to help the client reach optimum personal development so that he can handle himself and his problems, present or future, in a more mature and efficient manner. In the scholastic synthesis human maturity and efficiency in the natural order is epitomized in a perfection of the highest potential resource of man as it is related to action. In the concrete this is the practical intellect which is to be perfected and developed for directing and unifying human activity through the intellectual habit or virtue of prudence.

In the light of these facts it seems reasonable at this point to investigate the virtue of prudence as it is presented and understood by scholastic authorities. From this study it is hoped that both the philosophical and the psychological framework which is necessary for the scholastic evaluation and judgment of the controverted issues concerning the process of counseling can be constructed.

In his recently published book Charles A. Curran, a proponent of the client-centered school of counseling, treats of certain "limited implications" relevant to this problem.[67]

---

[67]Charles A. Curran, *Counseling in Catholic Life and Education* (New York: The Macmillan Company, 1952), pp. v-462.

CHAPTER IV

THE PHILOSOPHICAL SETTING FOR COUNSELING

Human Actions and Self-Mastery

It has become clear that the controlling aim of the counseling process is to assist others by specialized methods to become more effectively self-directive. Such a goal, however lofty and democratic it may sound, is of little real significance unless effective self-direction is both desirable and possible for men.

That self-direction is desirable most men would agree. That effective self-direction is truly possible for man many psychologists theoretically deny. This is evident from their express or implicit adherence to some form of determinism. These may range from the physical determinists who are as "old as Democritus and as young as Freud"[1] to the mental determinists who are found among the ancients or the moderns, such as Snygg and Combs.[2]

It is not quite accurate to classify Snygg and Combs as descendants of the mental determinists alone. It is closer to the truth if they are seen as descendants of both mental and physical determinists for they seem to embrace the errors of each. For them it is mind that determines but their mind does not rise above the level of sensibility and materiality. The central thesis of their "phenomenological frame of reference" for psychology is stated as follows: "All behavior, without exception, is completely determined by and pertinent to the phenomenal field of the behaving organism."[3]

Whether Snygg and Combs are ideological descendants of the physical or mental determinists it is evident that their

[1] Robert E. Brennan, O.P., *The Image of His Maker* (Milwaukee: The Bruce Publishing Co., 1948), p. 221.

[2] Donald Snygg and Arthur W. Combs, *Individual Behavior* (New York: Harper and Brothers, 1949), p. 386.

[3] *Ibid.*, pp. 15, 230.

brand of determinism is such that human freedom has no place in their "phenomenological" theory. They carefully note this position in the early part of their exposition.

As a science, phenomenological psychology must accept determinism because prediction and control are only possible in a field where behavior is lawful and caused. As a method, it also recognizes that the behaver often feels that he has a choice of behavior even though none exists in reality, since he always chooses the one which is pertinent to his phenomenal field at the instant of action.[4]

To Thomas Aquinas and those who follow him as he followed Aristotle, any species of physical or intellectual determinism that would destroy the essential freedom of the human will, the universal psychological motor within man's rational soul,[5] is without basis in fact and is consequently rejected. All such theories must of necessity make man less than he is and deny him his uniquely human rights, chief of which is his right to self-direction in his search for human happiness. On this point Farrell interprets the Thomistic teaching with skill and accuracy:

. . . if we are to get at the truth of human happiness, we cannot simply scramble human activity with every other form of action in the universe. To act for a goal of our own choosing, and that means to attempt to attain happiness, is a uniquely human right. Other things, other creatures, may be propelled toward a goal by the drive of physical necessity or of animal instinct, much as an arrow is shot toward a target by the impulse and aim of the archer. But only man can direct action towards a goal, for only man is in control of his actions. Control of action involves deliberate will, the ability to see the connection between the tools used and the job to be done, between means and end[6]

Both the intellect and the will, the apprehensive and the appetitive powers of the human soul that distinguish man from all creatures below him, have an essential function in the control and direction of all activity that is properly human. As Aquinas notes:

[4]*Ibid.*, p. 25.
[5]Thomas Aquinas, *Summa Theologica* (New York: Benziger Brothers, 1947), I, q. 82, a. 4; I-II, q. 9, a. 1, q. 17, a. 1.
[6]Walter Farrell, O.P., *A Companion to the Summa* (New York: Sheed and Ward, 1941), II, 7.

In man there are but two principles of human activity, viz., the intellect or reason and the appetite; for these are the two principles of movement in man.[7]

The function of the intellect is to know the truth. The function of the will is to desire, to move towards, and enjoy the good presented to it by the intellect.[8] The will of itself is blind, and as a consequence, it follows and is limited in its operation by knowledge. The intellect, left to itself, is incapable of movement and though always ready to apprehend the truth about the good, it lacks the power to grasp the good as good. The proper functioning of the intellect and the will are necessary to produce controlled and deliberate movement, or action with knowlelge, the only means man has to attain true human happiness. Action alone is insufficient for this quest. Knowledge alone is likewise insufficient. Only controlled movement, or directed action is properly human, and it alone can lead man to happiness. Movement or action that is not controlled is not human movement. On this Aquinas is most insistent.

Of actions done by man those are properly called human which are proper to man as man. Now man differs from irrational animals in this, that he is master of his actions. Wherefore actions are properly called human actions, of which man is master. Now man is master of his actions through his reason and his will; whence too, the free will is defined as the faculty and the will and reason. Therefore those actions are properly called human which proceed from a deliberate will. And if any other actions are found in man, they can be called *actions of a man*, but not properly *human* actions, since they are not proper to man as man.[9]

Though man is destined to be master of his actions he is not born with that mastery completed. He does have certain natural potentialities, "for nature is never deficient or wanting in things necessary,"[10] which will give him mastery over his actions once they are activated according to his proper mode of perfection. Until these potentialities are actualized his mastery remains but a potential perfection.

[7]*Summa Theologica*, I-II, p. 58, a. 3.
[8]Thomas Aquinas, Q.D. *De Virtutibus in Communi* (Turin: Marietti, 1942), Quaestio Unica, a. 5.
[9]*Summa Theologica*, I-II, q. 1, a. 1.
[10]Aquinas, Q.D. *De Virtutibus in Communi*, q. 1, a. 8, ad. 20.

For a thing is perfect in proportion to its state of actuality, because we call that perfect which lacks nothing of the mode of its perfection.[11]

Virtue and Human Self-Mastery

Self-mastery, like the happiness which it brings to man, does not just happen. Both must be earned by the exercise of man's proper function, the performance of deliberate or human actions. Not any human action will suffice for real mastery leading to happiness, but human actions in accord with the rational nature that dictates the mode of perfection that is proper to man.[12] This is to be virtuous for "acts of virtue are suitable to human nature, since they are according to reason."[13] It is also to be happy as Aristotle noted, for "happiness is an activity of the soul in accordance with perfect virtue."[14]

Man grows in self-mastery as he grows in virtue. Man approaches greater natural happiness as he becomes more virtuous and is able to direct his activity to the good of his nature.[15] Following St. Augustine, Aquinas defines natural or acquired virtue as "a good habit of the mind by which we live righteously, of which no one makes bad use."[16] He also makes frequent use of the Aristotelian definition of virtue: "virtue is that which makes its possessor good, and his work good likewise."[17]

As virtue is a kind of habit it is necessary to understand the Thomistic notion of habit in order to grasp the significance of virtue in man's attempt to become master of himself.

To make the exercise of reasonable human action more permanently effective, that is, uniform, prompt, and delightful, human reason must develop certain habits which have the nature of metaphysical determinants in his rational powers.[18]

---

[11]*Summa Theologica*, I, q. 4, a. 1.
[12]*Ibid.*, II-II, q. 47, a. 6.
[13]*Ibid.*, I-II, q. 54, a. 3.
[14]Aristotle, *Nicomachean Ethics, Basic Works* (ed.), Richard McKeon (New York: Random House, 1941), I, 13, 1102a5.
[15]Aquinas, Q.D. *De Virtutibus in Communi*, q. 1, a. 9, ad 6.
[16]*Summa Theologica*, I-II, q. 55, a. 4.
[17]*Ibid.*, II-II, q. 47, a. 4; I-II, q. 56, a. 3.
[18]Aquinas, Q.D. *De Virtutibus in Communi*, q. 1, a. 1.

Habits help the powers of man to operate with ease and facility. They are voluntarily acquired qualities which modify the rational powers by way of a quiescent form which remains in the powers and disposes them to their acts.

Habits are a necessity for man because of the natural indifference of his limitless rational powers which are by nature ordained to universal truth and universal goodness. Necessitated only by absolute truth and the perfect good, they must in actuality deal with particular truths and particular kinds of goodness. To accomplish this task the rational powers must be determined.

> The rational powers, which are proper to man, are not determined to one particular action but are inclined indifferently to many; and they are determined to acts by means of habits.[19]

The work of habit is to modify a man, to give definiteness to his limitless powers. In the Thomistic sense habit is a qualification of man disposing him well or badly either as to his nature itself or to the operations for which that nature exists.[20] As a disposition ordered to operation habit is always a voluntary qualification resulting from true self-determination. Habits that dispose man for good operations are called virtues, while habits that dispose man for evil are called vices.

Habit occupies an unusual intermediary position between what the Scholastics call potency and act. Aquinas notes that "habit stands midway between power and act."[21] In relation to the undetermined inactive intellect or will, habit is an active, perfecting principle bringing those powers one step closer to their ultimate perfection of action. In relation to the acts of the intellect and will, that is, actual knowing and willing, habit is itself a potentiality.

As a voluntary determination or modification of man, adding accidental form, a simple active principle, a disposition to act in a reasonable way to the undetermined rational powers of his nature, habit is not a passing quality but one that has a certain stability and permanence. It is in this sense that Aquinas

[19] *Summa Theologica*, I-II, q. 55, a. 1.
[20] *Ibid.*, I-II, q. 49, a. 4.
[21] *Ibid.*, q. 71, a. 3.

calls habit a second nature which man may acquire through his deliberate, conscious, and repeated efforts since "habit is that which one uses when he wills."[22]

The Thomistic notion of habit and its function in the perfection of human nature is well summed up by Bourke. It is to be noted that habit is not

... a mere automatic conditioning of a power as the modern term "habit" connotes, but the metaphysical growth of the basic potency for operation. It does not decrease the activity of the intellect, or tend toward the semi-conscious repetition of a routine action as is suggested in much of the recent literature of habituation. It does not diminish the element of voluntary control, or verge upon involuntary, automatic, and non-human activity. Rather it represents an increase in the power of the intellect and the will, a vital growth of originally imperfect potentialities. It is a metaphysical perfectant, heightening man's rational capacities to such an extent that he who acts with a habituated intellect and will approaches the optimum performance of the strongest and the most perfect human being.[23]

In the development of self-mastery man does not create his good habits out of nothing, but by his reason he orders and perfects certain forces of cognition and appetition that are a part of his specific and individual nature.[24] These natural capacities for virtue, commonly found in all men because of their specific nature but differing in relative strength and direction among individuals because of their individuality, can be organized into certain patterns of action. When right reason consciously, voluntarily, and consistently uses these aptitudes man attains master of himself.[25]

If this self-mastery is to be complete it should extend the influence of reason to all aspects of human activity. As a consequence man must develop good habits or virtues in all of his rational powers.[26] Man has both intellective and appetitive powers subject to the control and direction of reason and both

---

[22]*Ibid.*, q. 50, a. 5.
[23]Vernon J. Bourke, "The Role of Habitus in Thomistic Metaphysics of Potency and Act," *Essays in Thomism*, (ed.) E. Brennan (New York: Sheed and Ward, 1942), pp. 106-07.
[24]*Summa Theologica*, I-II, q. 51, a. 1; q. 63, a. 1.
[25]Aquinas, *Q.D. De Virtutibus in Communi*, q. 1, a. 8.
[26]*Ibid.*, a. 12.

of these must be perfected for good works by human virtues. As Aquinas notes, "Human virtue . . . an operative habit, is a good habit productive of good works."[27]

The good habits of the intellect, which is both speculative and practical, are called intellectual virtues. The good habits of the appetites are called moral virtues.[28] The intellectual are in a sense more excellent than the moral virtues because they perfect the more excellent human power. As virtues, however, the intellectual virtues, excepting prudence, are somewhat deficient since they confer mere aptness for good works and they do not guarantee the right use of the powers.[29] The moral virtues along with the intellectual virtue of prudence are more perfect as virtues[30] since they imply the rectification of the will, which puts "all the powers and habits to their respective uses."[31]

The intellect itself is perfected for the possession and contemplation of truth by the habits of understanding, knowledge, and wisdom.[32, 33] The same intellect is perfected for the practical work of making and doing by the habits of art and prudence.[34]

The appetites which are rational by participation includes the intellectual appetite or will,[35] which is perfected for operations in relation to others by the habit of justice, and the sensitive appetite.[36] The latter because of "an inborn attitude to obey the command of reason"[37] can also be perfected by virtues. The chief virtues of the sensitive appetite are the habits of temperance and fortitude.[38]

[27]*Summa Theologica*, I-II, q. 55, a. 3.
[28]*Ibid.*, q. 58, a. 3.
[29]*Ibid.*, q. 57, a. 1.
[30]*Ibid.*, q. 56, a. 3.
[31]*Ibid.*, q. 57, a. 1.
[32]*Ibid.*, a. 2.
[33]These intellectual virtues give man objective truth and a hierarchy of values. They are the primary concern of formal educational agencies.
[34]*Ibid.*, a. 3, a. 4.
[35]*Ibid.*, I, q. 82, a. 5.
[36]*Ibid.*, I-II, q. 60, a. 2.
[37]*Ibid.*, q. 50, a. 3.
[38]*Ibid.*, q. 60, a. 4.

According to the teaching of St. Thomas human self-mastery becomes an enjoyable, prompt, and easy reality for man in direct proportion to his development and growth in virtues which "perfect man in view of his doing good deeds.[39] He maintains this position for two reasons: first, because man's undetermined human powers are perfected in proportion to the possession of habitual principles of operation,[40] and secondly, because it is then possible for man to order and direct all of his actions by reason with consistent efficiency.[41, 42]

The Virtue of Prudence and Self-Mastery

Since self-mastery is a practical work it is the task of the practical intellect to direct human actions in the acquisition of self-mastery. The practical intellect is not a distinct power from the speculative intellect but they do differ in their purpose.[43] The speculative intellect directs what it apprehends to contemplation, while the practical intellect directs what it apprehends to operations, or things to be done or made by man.[44]

To function well the practical intellect, like all rational powers in man, must be perfected by habits. It is the work of two virtues, prudence and art, to dispose the practical intellect for good operations in making and doing. Though both of these virtues are concerned with the right reason of their objects,

[39] *Ibid.*, q. 58, a. 3.
[40] *Ibid.*, q. 55, a. 1.
[41] Aquinas, *Q.D. De Veritate* (Turin: Marrietti, 1942), q. 20, a. 2.

[42] In the supernatural order, man is elevated through grace to the divine plane of a supernatural goal. Grace is the foundation of supernatural life, and from it the supernatural potentialities flow, and in it they are perfected.

The intellect and will are elevated and ordered directly to God by the theological virtues of Faith (*Summa Theologica*, II-II, q. 16), Hope (*Ibid.*, 17-22), and Charity (*Ibid.*, q. 23-46).

The infused moral virtues, specifically distinct from the acquired moral virtues, dispose man to direct his appetites to his supernatural end.

The Gifts of the Holy Ghost (*Ibid.*, I-II, q. 68) complete the supernatural organism and make man readily responsive to the movements of God. They are wisdom (II-II, q. 45), understanding (*Ibid.*, q. 8), knowledge (*Ibid.*, q. 9), Counsel (*Ibid.*, q. 52), piety (*Ibid.*, q. 121), fortitude, (*Ibid.*, q. 39), and fear of the Lord (*Ibid.*, q. 19).

[43] Aquinas, *Q.D. De Veritate*, q. 3, a. 3.
[44] *Summa Theologica*, I, q. 79, a. 11.

the difference of these objects makes their distinctive work evident.

Art is the right reason of things to be made; whereas prudence is the right reason of things to be done. Now making and doing differ in that making is an action passing into outward matter, e.g., to built, to saw, etc.; whereas doing is an action abiding in the agent, e.g., to see, to will, and the like.[45]

In view of their different objects, one of which has its perfection of being in the doer himself, the other in an object other than self, it is evident that it is through the virtue of prudence rather than art that the practical intellect brings order into man's human actions leading to self-mastery.[46] Self-mastery and the happiness which it brings to man are not attatined by knowing how to make things well, a perfection due to art, but by knowing how to do things well in the actual performance of particular deeds.[47] This perfection of knowledge and wisdom in action can be attained only through the virtue of prudence since "active happiness is an act of prudence by which man governs himself and others."[48] Thus St. Thomas maintains, "it belongs to the ruling of prudence to decide in what manner and by what means man shall obtain the mean of reason in his deeds."[49]

The meaning of prudence. — According to the common estimation of men, prudence implies a certain facility of reason in selecting or adapting the right means to a desired goal. St. Thomas notes that if the goal desired by man is evil, masquerading as good, the efforts of reason to determine the means to attain it may be classified as false prudence, or "prudence of the flesh."[50] The cleverness that devises counterfeit or apparently true means to either a good or an evil end is called "craftiness."[51] True and perfect prudence always refers to the process of thinking out and commanding the right means to a good end, not a

---

[45]*Ibid.*, I-II, q. 57, a. 4.
[46]*Ibid.*, II-II, q. 50, a. 2, ad. 3.
[47]Aquinas, *Q.D. De Vitutibus in Communi*, q. 1, a. 6, ad. 1.
[48]*Ibid.*, a. 5.
[49]*Summa Theologica*, II-q. 47, a. 7.
[50]*Ibid.*, q. 55, a. 3.
[51]*Ibid.*, a. 4.

particular good end but the "good end of man's whole life; and this alone is prudence simply so-called."[52]

Whether this true and perfect prudence is taken as a general condition of the human mind or as a specific virtue with determinant matter, as St. Thomas prefers, it implies a certain rectitude of discretion in matters of action and is thus distinct from all other virtues[53] of both the intellectual and the moral order.[54]

For his precise notion of this practical virtue, St. Thomas depends upon the wisdom of early Christian writers as well as upon Aristotle. From St. Augustine he drew the essential notion that prudence is a kind of practical knowledge related to the goodness of human actions. St. Augustine had described prudence in these words: "Prudence is the knowledge of what to seek and what to avoid."[55]

From St. Isidore, he gathers something of the eminence of prudence and the important element of foresight in relation to the rectitude of action. Isidore had presented the prudent man "as one who sees as it were from afar, for his sight is keen, and he foresees the events of uncertainties."[56]

With his customary precision St. Thomas crystallizes Aristotle's classical reference to prudence as "a true and reasoned state of capacity to act with regard to the things that are good or bad for man"[57] in the well known formula, "Prudence is the right reason of things to be done."[58] Again after Aristotle, Aquinas refers to prudence as a kind of wisdom, "Prudence is wisdom about human affairs."[59, 60]

The nature of prudence. — All these notions of prudence clearly indicate that it is a perfection of the intellect. It is "practical knowledge," "foresight," "the right reason" of behavior, and "wisdom" about human affairs. Consequently it is not sur-

---

[52]*Ibid.,* q. 47, a. 13.
[53]*Ibid.,* I-II, q. 61, a. 4.
[54]*Ibid.,* II-II, q. 47, a. 5.
[55]*Ibid.,* a. 1, s.c.
[56]*Ibid.,* a. 1.
[57]Aristotle, *Nicomachean Ethics,* VI, 5, 1140b, 5 and 6.
[58]*Summa Theologica,* II-II, q. 46, a. 2, s.c.
[59]Aristotle, *op. cit.,* VI, 5, 1140b, 20 and 21.
[60]*Summa Theologica,* II-II, q. 47, a. 2, ad 1.

prising that St. Thomas maintains that prudence is "essentially an intellectual virtue."[61]

Prudence, however, is distinct from the other intellectual virtues. It differs from the speculative virtues of understanding, knowledge, and wisdom in that they are concerned with universal and necessary truth, while prudence has to do with singular and consequently contingent things. The object of prudence as an intellectual virtue is the truth about human actions in relation to human happiness.[62] As such prudence is always concerned with particular and contingent human acts that have their perfection of being in the doer himself, such as the acts of willing, seeing, desiring, choosing, and the like.[63]

St. Thomas also holds that the virtue of prudence, distinct by reason of its object from art, is even more practical than its companion virtue of the practical intellect. He agrees with Aristotle[64] in maintaining that the virtue of prudence is something more than a merely rational habit, as art can very well be since it is a perfection of judgment,[65] while prudence always includes the application of knowledge to action. This application is made with the help of the will.

> The worth of prudence consists not in thought, but in its application to action, which is the end of the practical reason.[66]

Understood in this light the virtue of prudence is seen as a bridge between the realm of thought and the realm of action, between the intellectual and the moral order. It is a perfection of man which demands the perfect cooperation of the two principles of all human action, the intellect and the will.

Prudence and the moral virtues. — Although prudence is formally an intellectual virtue perfecting the practical intellect for the direction of human action according to right reason, it is said to be materially moral since it is concerned with the matters of moral actions.[67] As the director of moral action,

---

[61]*Ibid.*, I-II, a. 3, ad 1.
[62]*Ibid.*, II-II, q. 47, a. 5, ad. 3.
[63]*Ibid.*, a. 3 and a. 5.
[64]Aristotle, *op. cit.*, VI, 5, 1140b 28.
[65]*Summa Theologica*, II-II, q. 47, a. 8.
[66]*Ibid.*, a. 1, ad. 3.
[67]*Ibid.*, I-II, q. 58, a. 3, ad 1.

prudence is closely related to the moral order, but it is not to be confused with the moral virtues. While it enjoys the perfection of virtue proper to moral virtues since it presupposes a rectified appetite[68] it is formally distinct from them. The moral virtues are perfections of the appetitive powers, while prudence is a perfection of the intellective power.[69] The moral virtues rightly dispose man toward the reasonable or good ends of human action which man naturally knows through the habit of first principles of action called synderesis.[70]

> Synderesis is said to be the law of the mind, because it is a habit containing the precepts of the natural law, which are the first principles of human action.[71]

It is in view of these naturally known ends of the moral virtues that the virtue of prudence has to do with the selection and the command of the right means to attain them.[72] St. Thomas speaks of the interrelation of prudence, the moral virtues, and synderesis in this way:

> The end concerns the moral virtues, not as though they appointed the end, but because they tend to the end which is appointed by natural reason. In this they are helped by prudence, which prepares the way for them, by disposing the means. Hence it follows that prudence is more excellent than the moral virtues, and moves them; yet synderesis moves prudence just as understanding of principles moves science.[73]

Right leaning toward human good and human happiness is the work of the moral virtues. The right selection and command of the suitable means to attain human good and human happiness through particular actions is the work of prudence. Human happiness is impossible without right moral action. It is impossible to produce the right moral action without the virtue of prudence. The action of prudence as an intellectual virtue proceeding from first principles is, in turn, impossible without the knowledge of the first principles of human action,

[68] *Ibid.*, q. 56, a. 2, ad. 3; II-II, q. 47, a. 4.
[69] *Ibid.*, II-II, q. 47, a. 5.
[70] *Ibid.*, a. 6.
[71] *Ibid.*, I-II, q. 94, a. 1, ad. 2.
[72] *Ibid.*, I-II, q. 58, a. 4.
[73] *Ibid.*, II-II, q. 47, a. 6, ad 3.

the ends of the moral virtues which are supplied by the habit of synderesis.

The acts of prudence. — As a determinant or perfectant of the practical intellect in relation to virtuous operations the habit of prudence must dispose the practical intellect to its perfection in act. The goal of the practical intellect is always action. There are three acts of the practical intellect in relation to things done by man. The first of these is counsel, the second is judgment, and the third is the command of action.

The first two of these acts, the acts of counsel and judgment, correspond to similar acts of the speculative intellect which are inquiry and judgment. The third, the act of command, is proper to the practical intellect as it is directly ordered to operations.[74] As operation or action is the goal of the practical intellect, that act is its principal act which comes closest to that goal. This is clearly the act of command to which the other two acts of counsel and judgment are subordinate. The act of command consists in the application to action of the things counseled and judged.[75] St. Thomas defines command as "an act of the reason, presupposing an act of the will, in virtue of which the reason, by its command moves to the execution of the act."[76]

It is the task of the virtue of prudence to dispose the practical intellect to command reasonably. To accomplish this it needs the help of other habits or virtues. These are the habits of good counsel (euboulia)[77] and good judgment (synesis and gnome).[78] Like the subordinate acts of the practical intellect which they determine, the virtues of good counsel and good judgment are subordinate to the principal virtue of human action, or prudence.

St. Thomas calls the subordinate virtues of good counsel and good judgment potential parts of the virtue of prudence and briefly explains their nature in relation to prudence.

[74]*Ibid.*, I-II, q. 57, a. 6.
[75]*Ibid.*, II-II, q. 47, a. 8.
[76]*Ibid.*, I-II, q. 17, a. 3.
[77]*Ibid.*, II-II, q. 51, a. 1 and 2.
[78]*Ibid.*, q. 51, a. 3 and 4.

The potential parts of a virtue are the virtues connected with it, which are directed to certain secondary acts or matters, not having, as it were, the whole power of the principal virtue. In this way the parts of prudence are good counsel, which concerns counsel, synesis, which concerns judgment in matters of ordinary occurrence, and gnome, which concerns judgment in matters of exception to the law; while prudence is about the chief act which is command.[79]

Counsel. — To command a prudent action, that is, to command the right means to attain a good end, is not an easy task. To know exactly what should be done in a particular situation of some concern in which there are several possibilities of action, is always difficult.[80] The end of human action, to live and act according to reason, or to be virtuous in all actions, is fixed by nature. About this end, when it is understood as an end, a good to be attained, there can be no doubt.[81]

With the selection and the command of the proper means to this end it is otherwise. Far from being fixed, the means to good and happiness in human affairs are, at least potentially, of an almost infinite variety according to the variety of persons, affairs, and circumstances.[82] Because human actions are about contingent singulars which by reason of their variability are uncertain, there is always much uncertainty about things that have to be done.[83] Uncertainty about actions gives rise to fear which disposes man to take counsel concerning the actions to be performed.[84]

As a consequence, before a man can proceed to the reasonable command of a particular action in matters that admit of doubt, he must take counsel. He may counsel with himself alone or with others. In these practical matters of human ac-

---

[79] *Ibid.*, q. 48, a. 1.
[80] *Ibid.*, I-II, q. 14, a. 4.
[81] *Ibid.*, q. 14, a. 2.
[82] *Ibid.*, II-II, q. 47, a. 15.
[83] *Ibid.*, I-II, q. 14, a. 1.
[84] *Ibid.*, q. 44, a. 2, ad 2. St. Thomas explains the effect of fear thus: "The stronger the passion is, the greater the hindrance it is to the man who is swayed by it. Consequently, when fear is intense man does indeed wish to take counsel, but his thoughts are so disturbed, that he can find no counsel. If, however, the fear be slight, so as to make a man wish to take counsel, without gravely disturbing reason, it may even make it easier for him to take good counsel, by reason of his ensuing carefulness."

tion experience is the great teacher. Experience tends to reduce the infinity of singulars about particular human actions to a finite number that occur as a general rule and knowledge of these is sufficient for prudent action.[85] As a consequence if a man's personal experience and knowledge are sufficient to dispel reasonable doubt about what should be done in a particular instance, his own counsel is sufficient. If not, as is often the case in significant personal difficulties with many attendant circumstances which can be considered by several people with greater certainty,[86] he must seek counsel from others more experienced and with greater knowledge. This act of counsel may be defined as an inquiry of the reason of that which is to be done. In doubtful and perplexing matters this act of counsel is most necessary to avoid the rash or precipitous actions[87] that are performed on the mere impulse of the will or passions. Of this act of the reasonable man St. Thomas speaks thus:

> Now in doubtful and uncertain things the reason does not pronounce judgment, without previous inquiry; wherefore the reason must of necessity institute an inquiry before deciding on the objects of choice; this inquiry is called counsel.[88]

To insure the rectitude of reason's counsel, the subject of which is the discovery of the right means to the end, the suitable time, place, mode, and extent of counsel in view of all the attendant circumstances surrounding particular human actions,[89] the practical intellect must be disposed by the virtue of good counsel or euboulia.[90] Since the act of counsel is directed to the act of command as that which is principal in relation to actions, the habit of good counsel has the nature of a virtue only in so far as it is directed to and by prudence as the principal virtue.[91] In somewhat technical language this idea is expressed by saying that to take good counsel belongs to the virtue of pru-

[85]*Ibid.*, II-II, q. 47, a. 3, ad 2.
[86]*Ibid.*, I-II, q. 14, a. 3.
[87]*Ibid.*, II-II, q. 53, a. 3.
[88]*Ibid.*, I-II, q. 14, a. 1.
[89]*Ibid.*, II-II, q. 51, a. 1, ad. 3.
[90]Aristotle, *op. cit.*, VI, 10, 1142b 16 and 21.
[91]*Summa Theologica*, II-II, q. 51, a. 2.

dence as commanding it, to euboulia as eliciting it.[92] In another place St. Thomas remarks more simply,

> Prudence makes us be of good counsel, not as though its immediate act consisted in being of good counsel but because it perfects the latter act by means of a subordinate virtue which is euboulia.[93]

Judgment. — Though good counsel concerning the means to a good end is a most important prerequisite for prudential commands it alone is not sufficient. The counsel is not effectively complete until the practical reason has made a judgment or decision on the counseled means in relation to man's proposed activity.[94] This act of judgment brings the counsel to a close and results in certitude about the means to be used in a particular action.[95]

As counsel and judgment are different acts of the practical reason they must be disposed to good action by different habits or virtues. That goodness of judgment and goodness of counsel are not due to the same cause is evident from the fact that "many can take good counsel, without having good sense to judge well."[96] This lack of good "sense" may arise from a deficiency in the powers of the intellect or senses, or from a bad disposition in these powers. In either case a distorted apprehension of reality results. This distortion is directly due to the lack of true and correct ideas in the intellect, and indirectly to the evil disposition of the appetite which is not rectified in relation to right ends, the particular principles of action.[97]

Right judgment concerning the ends of human action is assured by the moral virtues which rectify the appetite and moderate the passions[98] for the virtuous man judges "aright of

---

[92] *Ibid.*, ad 2.
[93] *Ibid.*, I-II, q. 57, a. 6, ad 1.
[94] Thomas de Vio Cajetan, *Commentarium in Summa Theologicam*, Leonine ed. (Rome: 1888-1906), I-II, q. 14, a. 1.
[95] *Summa Theologica*, II-II, q. 51, a. 2, ad 2.
[96] *Ibid.*, a. 3.
[97] *Ibid.*, a. 3, ad 1.
[98] The passions or emotions to be moderated by the moral virtues are extensively treated by St. Thomas in the *Summa Theologica*, I-II, q. 22-48. The tract is on the passions in general (q. 22-25), and in particular (q.26-48). Among the latter he treats of love, hatred, desire, joy, sorrow, hope and despair, courage and anger.

the end of virtue, because 'such as a man is, such does the end seem to him' as noted in the 3rd Ethics."[99]

St. Thomas explains the effect of emotions on the judgment of reason:

> ... the judgment and apprehension of reason is impeded on account of a vehement and inordinate apprehension of the imagination and judgment of the estimative power, as appears in those who are out of their mind.
> Now it is evident that the apprehension of the imagination and the judgment of the estimative power follows the passion of the sensitive appetite, even as the verdict of taste follows the disposition of the tongue, for which reason we observe that those who are in some kind of passion do not easily turn their imagination away from the object of their emotion, the result being that the judgment of reason often follows the passion of the sensitive appetite, and consequently the will's movement follows it also, since it has a natural inclination to follow the judgment of reason.[100]

St. Thomas finds that two virtues are necessary to prevent distortion in the cognitive power and provide the true and correct ideas for reasonable judgment. These virtues help man avoid the inconsideration which may arise from contempt or neglect of those things on which right judgment depends.[101] While good counsel is insured by one virtue, two are necessary for good judgment because of two different rules on which right judgment may be based, i.e., the common law and the natural law. After Aristotle the two virtues of good judgment are called by their Greek names of *synesis* (common sense) and *gnome* (extraordinary judgment).[102]

> Synesis judges of actions according to the common law; while gnome bases its judgments on the natural law in those cases where the common law fails to apply.[103]

The two virtues of good judgment, which disposes the reason to judge well in matters of counsel with reference to human action, like the virtue of good counsel, have the nature of virtues inasmuch as they are directed to and by the virtue of pru-

---

[99] Aristotle, *op. cit.*, III, 5 1140a 30.
[100] *Summa Theologica*, I-II, q. 77, a. 1.
[101] *Ibid.*, II-II, q. 53, a. 4.
[102] Aristotle, *op. cit.*, VI, 11, 1143a 10, 19 sq.
[103] *Summa Theologica*, I-II, q. 57, a. 6, ad 3.

dence. Good judgment is commanded by prudence through the virtues of synthesis and gnome.

Command and the perfection of prudence. — The perfection of the virtue of prudence is not realized until good counsel and good judgment are applied to action. To avoid inconsistancy,[104] delay, or negligence,[105] in the application of knowledge to action the practical intellect needs the virtue of prudence to determine its principal act of command. Right action demands more than right thinking about what is to be done. Reasonable command of action is also necessary. "To command," says St. Thomas, "is nothing else than to direct someone to do something by a certain motion of intimation."[106] The proper and immediate act of the virtue of prudence is to command the execution of what should be done here and now to attain a good end.[107] Command results in effective, orderly movement.

The virtue of prudence is more eminent than the virtues of good judgment, just as the latter is more eminent than the virtue of good counsel. The inquiry of counsel is directed to judgment as its end, and judgment is directed to command of action.[108] A man is not prudent merely because he counsels well and always judges well. A prudent man is a man of action who accomplishes in deed the things that have to be done in the way in which reason dictates that they should be done. To do this good counsel and good judgment are necessary but above all the commanding virtue of prudence is required. As St. Thomas notes,

Prudence is a virtue most necessary for human life. For a good life consists in good deeds. Now in order to do good deeds, it matters not only what a man does, but also how he does it; to wit, that he does it from right choice and not merely from impulse or passion.[109]

It is through the prudent command of action that man becomes the master of himself. Anything that interferes with prudential command interferes with man's mastery of his own life.

[104]*Ibid.*, II-II, q. 53, a. 6.
[105]*Ibid.*, II-II, q. 54, a. 2, ad 3.
[106]*Ibid.*, I-II, q. 17, a. 2.
[107]Aristotle, *op. cit.*, VI, 9, 1239.
[108]*Ibid.*, 1240.
[109]*Summa Theologica*, I-II, q. 57, a. 5.

It makes no difference whether that interference comes from within his nature or without. When a man's ability to command his actions weakens, he has begun to turn over the direction of his life to someone or something else. Uncontrolled or inordinate passions, the delay of laziness, the negligence of complacency, the wavering of inconstancy, all militate against the integrity of man's reasonable command. Each makes a direct attack upon his ability to be master of himself. Conversely, whatever strengthens his reasonable command of action builds up his power of self-mastery. It is of little importance whether the reasonable commands of man are respected by others or not. What is important for self-mastery and human happiness is that the commands of reason be supreme within man's own soul. This supremacy of reasonable command and the perfection of self-mastery resulting in human happiness is assured by the virtue of prudence.

The integral parts of prudence. — Besides the subordinate virtues of good counsel and good judgment which perfect the subordinate or commanded acts of prudence, the formal perfection of the virtue demands many other conditions (dispositions, functions, or acts) in the production of reasonable commands. Borrowing from the physical order, St. Thomas refers to these conditions as integral[110] or quasi-integral parts of the virtue.[111] These are "the things which need to concur for the perfect act of the virtue."[112] The term *integral* is used metaphorically in this connection so the integral parts are not to be considered as constituting the principal virtue but as necessary conditions disposing man for the acquisition and exercise of the acts of the principal virtue. They have a double purpose. The integral parts both remove all obstacles to the operation of the principal virtue and assist in its perfect operation.

St. Thomas finds that there are eight conditions or integral parts necessary to dispose a man for the perfection of prudential operations. He presents them as they are related to knowledge.[113] Since human acts are concerned with contingent

---

[110]*Ibid.*, II-II, q. 48, a. 1.
[111]*Ibid.*, q. 49, a. 1.
[112]*Ibid.*, q. 48, a. 1. Cf. also q. 143, a. 1.
[113]*Ibid.*

singulars, man must know a great deal about them before he can order his actions with any degree of certainty. He must also know the universal principles of right action which are to be applied to the particular situations in doubt.[114] In the absence of this knowledge the right means to a desired end are lost in the fog of obscurity and darkness. Search for them can only result in confusion. Under such conditions the reasonable, orderly action which is the perfection of prudence is impossible. It is the task of the integral parts of prudence to supply for this deficiency or rather to do away with it altogether and to overcome the obstacles in the way of its perfect operation.

St. Thomas first considers the five integral parts that are necessary for prudence as a cognitive virtue.[115] These are memory, reasoning, understanding, docility and sagacity. Something of the distinctive contribution that each of these integral parts makes for the perfection of prudence can be seen in relation to three conditions of knowledge. The first is knowledge itself: if it is of the past it is called *memory;* if it is of the present, either particular or universal, it is called *understanding* or insight. The second is the acquisition of knowledge: if it is caused by teaching *docility* is required; if it is caused by discovery *sagacity* is necessary. The third is the use of knowledge: for this the process of *reasoning* is necessary to proceed from things known to knowledge or judgment of other things.

Three other integral parts are necessary for the perfection of that which is proper and formal to prudence as commanding or applying knowledge to action.[116] These are foresight, circumspection, and caution, the necessary conditions of right command. The order of right means to a good end demands *foresight*. Attention to all the circumstances of the particular matter at hand demands *circumspection*. To avoid unforeseen obstacles *caution* is a necessity.

A more penetrating analysis of the nature of these integral parts of prudence as well as their relation to the potential parts and the commanded acts of prudential operations will be attempted in the following chapter.

[114]*Ibid.,* q. 47, a. 3.
[115]*Ibid.,* q. 48, a. 1.
[116]*Ibid.*

CHAPTER V

THE PSYCHOLOGICAL SETTING FOR COUNSELING

The Acquisition of Prudence and Moral Virtue

The acquisition of virtue in general. — The good habits that are necessary to make man a worthy citizen of the natural world and to attain natural perfection do not exceed the powers of human nature. Man has within his specific and individual nature a natural aptitude to virtue and the limited human happiness which the perfect possession of these good habits will bring to him. In the pursuit of natural perfection the potentialities of man are more extensive than those of the creatures below him. The latter are limited or determined to one mode of operation by their forms but they also possess a natural passive aptitude to certain other perfections that may be acquired by the action of an exterior agent. They cannot determine themselves in any way. Man, on the other hand, has by nature undetermined rational powers with a natural aptitude for human virtues that he can activate and bring to perfection by his own action.[1]

This possibility of true self-determination is enjoyed by man because he has within his soul as part of his natural equipment both active and passive principles of action. In the operation and the interaction of the intellect and will there is always an element of passivity. The intellect moves the will and the will moves the intellect. Both are what St. Thomas calls "moved movers."[2] In the intellect itself an active element, the agent intellect, is responsible for the movement of a passive element, the receptive intellect for the act of intellection.[3] The intellect in act, actually apprehending and judging, moves the will by presenting its object, "for the good understood is the end that moves the apetite."[4] The will moved by reason moves the sensitive appetite which by nature tends to obey reason.[5]

---

[1] Aquinas, *Q.D. De Virtutibus in Communi*, q. 1, a. 9.
[2] *Summa Theologica*, I-II, q. 51, a. 2.
[3] *Ibid.*, I, q. 79, a. 4, ad 4.
[4] Aquinas, *Q.D. De Virtutibus in Communi*, q. 1, a. 9.
[5] *Summa Theologica*, I-II, q. 50, a. 3.

Through the voluntary, conscious use of his active and passive principles of action man can generate inclinations to act in a certain and definite way within his rational and rationally controlled powers. The natural potentiality of these powers to act in a variety of ways remains, but through repeated actions they are disposed by an accidental form to operate in a definite direction. By the repetition of deliberate acts inclining the human powers to act in a reasonable way a good disposition is established in them. When this good disposition is voluntarily and consistently used in the production of good actions it grows more fixed until the virtue is firmly established.[6]

To eliminate from human habits their distinctively human characteristic of voluntariness is to destroy their meaning and value in the process of self-perfection. To consider human habits or virtues in any other way than as voluntarily acquired qualities modifying the powers of the soul, disposing those powers for their perfection in act, is to fail to understand their significant contribution to human living. Human habit is always subject to the will in operation.[7] Through human habits the powers of the intellect, the will, and the sensitive appetites are channeled into freely selected patterns of action. It is under the reasonable command of the practical intellect that each individual regulates the extensiveness of his development and growth in the habitual principles of virtuous living.

As noted above, nature and the Author of nature give the human agent its start in virtuous living. This start amounts to a push in the right direction and the power to carry on.[8] Beyond this nature does not go. The development of his natural potentiality for virtue is left to the individual himself. Personal effort in the repetition of reasonable personal acts is the efficient cause of all human virtues.

Certain habits or virtues of the intellect can be generated by a single act of the reason, since the passive power of the intellect can be entirely overcome by an active element. Such is the case in the generation of the habit of understanding which

[6] *Ibid.*, q. 51, a. 2.
[7] *Ibid.*, q. 49, a. 3; q. 50, a. 5.
[8] *Ibid.*, q. 51, a. 1; q. 63, a. 1.

contains the first principles of thought and action, and the generation of the habit of science from self-evident propositions.

The generation of virtues in the appetitive power is more difficult and always requires many acts of the reason. The natural indeterminacy and the variety of objects that appeal to the human appetite prevent its being overcome by a single judgment of the reason concerning what should be willed. It is only by repeated acts that the reason can determine the appetite to a single manner of operation. Until this uniform inclination is firmly established there is no habituation and consequently no virtue, for habits of virtue like a second nature incline the powers to uniformity of action in the majority of cases.[9]

Since habits are a kind of form, a simple, immaterial, indivisible active principle, it is clear that they do not increase in magnitude as material things, by the addition of quantity to quantity. Habits become greater when they become more perfect. This happens either when they extend to more things, as knowledge is said to be greater when it includes more objects, or when it penetrates more deeply in the subject, as equal knowledge is more firmly grasped by one than another.[10] As an habitual determination of the human powers the perfection of a virtue arises either from its extension to more things or from deeper penetration in the power.

Though virtuous habits are caused by virtuous acts, not every act of virtue perfects the habit of virtue. Virtuous acts that are remiss or deficient in intensity to the disposition or habit from which they flow do not dispose to the increase but rather to a decrease in the perfection of virtue. Virtuous acts equal in intensity to the disposition or habit from which they flow dispose the habit for an increase, while it is actually made more perfect by acts of greater intensity.[11]

The acquisition of total prudence. — The virtue of prudence as a habit of reason is a firm disposition to right action perfecting the practical intellect. As noted above the value of prudence in the search for human happiness does not consist in right thinking alone, but rather in the application of right think-

[9]*Ibid.*, q. 51, a. 3.
[10]*Ibid.*, q. 52, a. 1.
[11]*Ibid.*, q. 52, a. 3.

ing to the direction of human actions. For this application the practical intellect and its perfection of prudence needs the immediate assistance of the will, the efficient psychological motor of all human activity.[12]

The perfection of prudence in the direction of human actions, which consists in commanding the right means to good ends, is impossible unless the will of man is well inclined both to the reasonable ends of human living and the means of attaining those ends. The end or good understood is the immediate object of the will. To this end the will freely tends in virtue of its natural inclination when it is presented by the intellect. The practical intellect perfected by prudence is directly concerned with the consideration and command of the right means to the good ends that are already known by the intellect (synderesis) and desired by a well inclined (moral virtues in intention) will. The right desire or intention of a good end is thus presupposed to the action of prudence. The good as end must be understood by the intellect and intended by the will before the practical intellect through the virtue of prudence institutes the process of counseling, judging, and commanding the right means to attain it.[13, 14, 15]

Because of the close relationship and the interdependence of the intellect and the will in the production of human actions perfect prudence and the perfection of moral virtue are acquired at the same time. As St. Thomas notes,

> The acquired virtues are caused by intention; and it is necessary that they be caused at once in the man, who proposes to acquire one virtue; and he shall not acquire them, unless at the same time he acquires prudence, with which all are had.[16]

In the acquisition of perfect and total prudence man must repeatedly exercise his practical intellect in the acts of good counsel, judgment, and command of the right means to the

[12]*Ibid.*, II-II, q. 47, a. 1, ad 3; I, q. 82, a. 4.

[13]*Ibid.*, I-II, q. 58, a. 5, ad 5.

[14]Peter Lumbreras, *De Habitibus et Virtutibus in Communi* (Rome: Collegio Angelico, 1950), n. 181, p. 115.

[15]John of St. Thomas, *Cursus Theologicus*, Vives ed. (Paris: 1885), I-II, disp. 16, a. 4.

[16]Aquinas, *Q.D. De Virtutibus Cardinalibus*, q. 1, a. 2.

"good end of man's whole life."[17] His well disposed will must cooperate with its acts of consent, choice, and use which results in the perfection of the moral virtues. Total prudence and perfect moral virtues are inseparable companions in the quest for human happiness.[18] Neither can exist as perfect natural habits or virtues without the other[19] When a man acquires the perfection of prudence, the ability to consider and command the right means to the good end of human life in all his actions, he has also acquired the moral virtues that are necessary for his total and perfect moral rectification.[20,21]

By the repetition of good counsel, judgment, and command, man generates the virtue of prudence in his practical reason. By frequent consent to the counseled means, good choice, and use he generates the moral virtues in his appetitive powers.[22] In the beginning these virtues are generated as dispositions, prudence is partial and the moral virtues imperfect. After long and frequent exercise in the acts of these virtues, there will come a time when one more act will be sufficient to generate these virtues as habits. When this act is exercised prudence and perfect moral virtue result.[23] Lumbreras treats this problem clearly in the following statement:

[17]*Summa Theologica*, II-II, q. 47, a. 13.
[18]*Ibid.*, I-II, q. 58, a. 4; q. 73, a. 1, ad. 1.
[19]*Ibid.*, I-II, q. 65, a. 1; II-II, q. 47, a. 5, ad 1 and 2.
[20]Thomas Aquinas, *Commentarium in Decem Libros Ethicorum Aristotelis* (Turin: Marietti, 1934), VI, 11. Cf. also, *Summa Theologica*, I-II, q. 60, a. 1, ad 1; q. 57, a. 4, ad 3; q. 58, a. 2, ad 4; q. 65 ,a. 1, ad 3 and 4.
[21]The total rectification of the will for social living would include all of the moral virtues. These are extensively treated by St. Thomas in the *Summa Theologica*: *Justice* (II-II, q. 57-122), religion (q. 81-100), piety and patriotism (q. 101), observance (q. 102-03), obedience (q. 104-05), gratitude (q. 106-07), veracity (q. 109-13), affability (q. 114-16), and liberality (q. 117-19).
The rectification of the sensitive appetites for personal rectitude would include the virtues of *Fortitude* (II-II, q. 123-40), magnanimity (q. 129-33), magnificence (q. 34-35), patience (q. 136), perseverance (q. 137-138), and *Temperance* (II-II, q. 141-70), abstinence (q. 146-48), sobriety (q. 149-50), chastity (q. 151), virginity (q. 152), and continence (q. 155-56), meekness, (q. 157-59), modesty (q. 160-69), humility (q. 161-62), and studiousness (q. 166-67). [The cardinal virtues are italicized.]

[22]Fridalino Utz, *De Connexione Virtutum Moralium inter se secundum doctrinum St. Thomas Aquinatis* (Vechta in Oldenburg: Albertus-Magnus Verlag der Dominikaner, 1937), p. 124.

[23]Aquinas, *Q. D. De Virtutibus in Communi*, q. 1, a. 9, ad 11.

This ultimate act, which means a new command, a new election, and a new execution, by its own force and the force of previous acts, perfects not only the moral virtue by which it is elicited but also the virtue of prudence and the rest of the virtues connected with prudence. The subsequent right judgment, command, good election, and execution will come from the virtue, and hence they will be performed with promptness, ease, and pleasure. If because of many evil acts or the generation of a contrary habit, a moral virtue falls away from its perfection or is corrupted as a habit then simultaneously, total prudence and all the other perfect moral virtues are corrupted.[24]

Interaction of Intellect and Will in Prudential Operation

As noted before, the intellect and the will actively cooperate in all prudential activity. The extent of this cooperation is made more evident by the consideration of the various acts of both the intellect and the will in any human action. There are certain motions of the intellect and will to the end or good in human action that are presupposed to prudential activity. Prudence does not concern itself with the end but only with the determination of the means to a previously apprehended and desired goal. The interaction of the intellect and the will in reference to these are ordered and directed by the virtue of prudence.

Analysis of human action shows that there are twelve interrelated acts of the intellect and the will involved in any human activity. These acts may be classified in three orders, the order of desire, the order of choice, and the order of execution.

Order of desire. — As nothing is desired or willed unless it is known all human action must begin with an act of the intellect and thus it is with the origin of the order of desire.

The intellect must first apprehend some goal or end and present it as a good to the will. This act of the intellect is a value *judgment* of what it apprehends.[25] The will by its nature reacts to this goal or good with a simple volition, a natural com-

[24]Peter Lumbreras, O.P., "Notes on the Connection of the Virtues," *The Thomist*, II (1948), 226.

[25]Reginald Garrigou-Lagrange, O.P., "La prudence dans l'organisme de vertus," *Revue Thomiste*, XXXI (1926), 240.

placency in the good presented which amounts to a mild interest or concern, an inefficacious desire.[26] This motion of the will is sufficient to move the intellect to judge whether or not this goal or good is attainable and worth striving for here and now. An affirmative *judgment* of the intellect arouses an efficacious desire or longing in the will which is an inclination to the good as a goal through certain means.[27] This act of the will is called *intention* and provides the motive power for an inquiry into the means to attain it.

The order of choice. — The act of intention in the will overflows from the order of desire and institutes the order of choice. By virtue of its intention the will moves the intellect to investigate or *counsel* about the suitable means to the desired goal.[28] The act of counsel in the intellect discovers the various means to the end and submits them to the will for *consent*.[29] The approval of the will in its act of consent to the means in general moves the intellect to determine which is the best and the most useful means to be used here and now to attain the desired goal. This act of *judgment*[30] in the intellect concerning the best means determines an act of *choice* in the will,[31] or the acceptance of the best means by the will.

The order of execution. — After the will has made a choice the motive force of that choice moves the intellect to *command* the execution or realization of the chosen means, and this act initiates the order of execution.[32] The will corresponds with an act called *active use*,[33] which applies the executing powers to their respective tasks in effecting the chosen means. *Passive use* in the powers subject to the will (intellect, senses, and motor powers) execute the means and attain the desired goal, resulting in *fruition,* happiness or joy in the will as it gains the goal or end desired.[34]

[26]*Summa Theologica*, I-II, q. 15, a. 3.
[27]*Ibid.*, q. 12, a. 1, ad 4; a. 4, ad 3.
[28]*Ibid.*, q. 14, a. 1, ad 1.
[29]*Ibid.*, q. 15, a. 3, ad 3.
[30]*Ibid.*, q. 17, a. 3, ad 1.
[31]*Ibid.*, q. 13, a. 1, ad 2; a. 3.
[32]*Ibid.*, q. 17, a. 1; a. 3, ad 1.
[33]*Ibid.*, q. 16, a. 1; q. 17, a. 3, ad 1 and 2.
[34]*Ibid.*, q. 11, a. 1.

Prudence as a virtue directly perfects the acts of counsel, judgment, and command in the practical intellect, and indirectly the acts of choice and active use in the will which it actively orders and directs. The relative position of these intellectual and volitional acts concerning the means can be observed more clearly in relation to the acts of the intellect and the will in reference to the end as they are presented on the following page.

Of the twelve acts involved in the deliberation and execution of human action, six pertain to the intellect and six to the will. Two acts of the intellect, apprehension, and judgment, are concerned with the end of human action, and four, counsel, practical judgment, command, and passive use have to do with the means. In the will there are three acts about the end, simple volition, intention, and fruition, and three are concerned with the means, consent, choice, and active use.

It is in the act of *command* alone that the intellect seems to share in a very intimate way in the efficient causality of the will.[35] In this act the intellect is capable of causing an impression or determination in the will, and by means of this determination in the other powers subject to the motion of the will. The intellect enjoys this efficiency because of the previous act of the will, the motive power of which carries over into the act of command elicited from the intellect.[36]

FUNCTIONAL ASPECTS OF PRUDENTIAL ACTS AND THE INTEGRAL PARTS

As previously noted there are three acts of the practical intellect to be disposed for right action by the virtue of prudence. These are the acts of counsel, judgment, and command. While reasonable command of action is elicited from the virtue of prudence as its chief act, good counsel and good judgment are pre-

[35]*Ibid.*, II-II, 83, a. 1.
[36]Aquinas, *Quaestiones Quodlibitales* (Paris: 1872), Vives ed., Quod. 9,

ACTS OF INTELLECT AND WILL IN HUMAN DELIBERATION AND EXECUTION
ORDER OF DESIRE

Acts of Intellect	Acts of Will
1. Apprehension of end as good, a value judgment;	2. Simple *volition* to good presented, inefficacious desire;
3. Judgment of attainability and worth of end;	4. Intention of end through the means, efficacious desire.

ORDER OF CHOICE

5. *Counsel* or investigation of the means to attain end;	6. *Consent* or approval of the means in general;
7. *Practical judgment* of this means as the best and to be used;	8. *Choice* or acceptance of this means which seems best.

ORDER OF EXECUTION

9. *Command* or orderly, effective movement to the execution of the chosen means;	10. *Active use* or the application of the executive powers to the task;
11. *Passive use* by which the intellect and the other powers carry out their operations;	12. *Fruition,* happiness or joy in the will resulting from the attainment of the desired end.

The action of the intellect upon the will is always, with one exception, operating in the order of final and formal causality. The will operates as an efficient cause, applying and giving motion to the intellect and the other powers as they move toward the goal or end of action.[37]

[37]*Ibid.*, I, q. 82, a. 4.

supposed to this principal act. As secondary or commanded acts of prudence good counsel and good judgment are elicited from the potential parts of prudence or the virtues of good counsel (euboulia), common sense (synesis), and extraordinary judgment (gnome).

As necessary conditions for the perfection of these three acts of prudence, St. Thomas enumerates eight integral parts. For its cognitive role prudence needs the assistance of reason, memory, understanding, sagacity, and docility. In its chief task of applying knowledge to actions the necessary conditions for prudential command are foresight, circumspection, and caution. An understanding of the nature of these eight integral parts and their relationship to the acts of prudence will help to clarify the function of the practical virtue in the direction of human operations. As necessary conditions they must be observed in the acquisition and exercise of prudence. Without the help of the integral parts the virtue of prudence is not possible.

Reason. — As a perfection of the practical intellect in relation to right operation the habit of prudence is subjected in reason. Thus it may seem unnecessary to specify *reason* as a necessary condition for the virtue of prudence. St. Thomas clearly indicates that as an integral part of prudence reason is to be understood as the ability to use the power of reason well and not as the power in which it resides.[38] Good use of reason is particularly necessary for the act of counsel and its completion in the act of judgment. Searching for the right means to a desired goal and the decision that determines the means to be used here and now is properly a process of reasoning which is completed when a judgment is made concerning that which should be done.

The ability to reason well is most necessary for prudential counsel because of the incertitude of the contingent and particular matters with which it is concerned. To apply universal and certain principles of action to the variable, singular elements of contingent human actions with any degree of certitude demands well developed reasoning power. Without good deductive reasoning about things to be done the virtue of pru-

[38] *Summa Theologica,* II-II, q. 49, a. 5, ad 1.

dence is impossible.[39] Because of the special need for good reasoning in prudential matters it is specified among the integral parts of the virtue.

> Prudence above all requires that man be an apt reasoner, so that he may rightly apply universals to particulars, which latter are various and uncertain.[40]

Memory. — If man must reason well to produce prudential actions he must have knowledge about the situation of which he reasons. Determining what should be done in a particular instance demands knowledge of both the universal principles of action and the singular matter about which the action is concerned.[41] The universal principles that govern the rightness or wrongness of all actions are naturally known and always available in the natural habit of synderesis.[42, 43] The applicatiton of these universal principles of right action varies in the particular and contingent situations of individual human actions. Through

---

[39]St. Thomas notes that inordinate and unmodified passion can corrupt or destroy the power of reason altogether. He also notes other effects of passion upon reason in the following passages.
Summa Theologica, I-II, q. 77, a. 2. "First, by way of distraction; secondly, by way of opposition, because passion often inclines to something contrary to what man knows in general; thirdly, by way of bodily transmutation, the result . . . is that reason is somehow fettered so that it cannot exercise its act freely . . .
Ibid., I-II, q. 77, a. 7. ". . . sometimes . . . the passion is not such as to take away the use of reason altogether; and then reason can drive the passion away, by turning to other thoughts, or it can prevent it from having its full effect; since the members are not put to work except by the consent of reason . . .
Ibid., I, q. 81, a. 3. ". . . the irascible and concupiscible appetites are said to obey reason. Anyone can experience this for himself; for by applying certain universal considerations, anger or fear or the like may be modified or excited.
Ibid., ad 2. "The intellect or reason is said to rule the irascible and the concupiscible by politic power; because the sensitive appetite has something in virtue of which it can resist the commands of reason. . . . And so from the fact that the irascible and the concupiscible resist reason in something, we must not conclude that they do not obey reason."

[40]*Ibid.,* II-II, q. 49, a. 5, ad 2.

[41]*Ibid.,* II-II, q. 47, a. 3.

[42]*Ibid.,* a. 6.

[43]*Ibid.,* I-II, q. 94, a. 21 ad 2. "As to those general principles, the natural law, in the abstract, can in no wise be blotted out from men's hearts. But it is blotted out in the case of a particular action, in so far as reason is hindered from applying the general principles to a particular point of practice on account of concupiscence or some other passion. . . . but as to the other, i.e., the secondary precepts, the natural law can be blotted out from the human heart, either by evil persuasions . . . or by vicious customs and corrupt habits. . . ."

experience, and experience alone, it is possible to determine how they are to be rightly applied in the majority of cases.[44] The retention, recall, and recognition of this experience is most important for prudential actions. A clear memory of past experience, of past counsels, previous judgments and commands that comprise experience in matters of action[45] is an irreplaceable assistant to prudential living. Knowledge of personal or vicarious experience retained in memory, recalled and recognized as pertinent in the actual consideration and determination of future action is an integral part, a necessary condition for the acquisition and exercise of the virtue of prudence.[46]

It behooves us to argue about the future from the past; wherefore memory of the past is necessary in order to take good counsel for the future.[47]

Understanding. — Besides the knowledge of past experience in matters of action supplied by memory, prudential consideration and decision demands clear knowledge and an accurate estimate of the present situation confronting man. Prudential action proceeds from a comparison of the present with the past to arrive at certitude concerning future action. It is thus that prudential foresight is to be developed through hindsight and insight. Memory takes care of the past. The accurate estimate of the present situation is furnished by the integral part of prudence called Understanding.[48]

St. Thomas carefully notes that as a necessary condition of the virtue of prudence *understanding* does not refer to the intellectual power itself, but rather to a right estimate of some particular and contingent matter of action.[49] Understanding always implies an intimate penetration of the truth,[50] and as an integral part of prudence it signifies an accurate vision of the present situation in view of the general moral principles that govern it. This discriminating awareness of the present situa-

[44] *Ibid.*, II-II, q. 49, a. 1.
[45] *Ibid.*, II-II, q. 47, a. 16, ad 2.
[46] *Ibid.*, q. 49, a. 1.
[47] *Ibid.*, ad 3.
[48] *Ibid.*, a. 2.
[49] *Ibid.*, ad 1.
[50] *Ibid.*, q. 8, a. 1; q. 49, a. 5.

tion in relation to the universal principles of action is properly an *insight*.

Prudential reasoning, like all deductive reasoning, proceeds from certain primary premises or understandings. There is a double understanding operative in the process of prudence leading to the practical conclusions about contingent matters of action. The first is universal and is supplied by the intellectual virtue through which man naturally knows the primary principles of action (synderesis), such as "do good" and "avoid evil."[51] This understanding provides the major premise of the prudential or practical syllogism. Though this premise is not always consciously expressed it must always operate in prudential reasoning.

The second understanding, which is necessary to form the minor premise of the practical syllogism, is particular, and consists in an accurate estimation of the here-and-now situation. The penetrating insight into the present contingent and singular matter of action depends in part upon the right operation of the sensitive cognitive power.[52, 53] This is an internal sense participating in reason, "whereby we judge of a particular."[54]

Insight includes a clear knowledge of a singular good as it is related to the universal principle that governs it. From this knowledge of the singular good proposed in the minor premise prudential reasoning draws the conclusion concerning what is to be done here and now.[55] The conclusion is the practical judgment leading to choice.

[51]*Ibid.*, I-II, q. 94, a. 1, ad 2; q. 94, a. 2.
[52]The perfection of the cogitative power is obtained with the moral virtues and then it estimates as good those things which are in accord with the rectified individual nature.
[53]*Ibid.*, I, q. 81, a. 3.
[54]*Ibid.*, II-II, q. 49, a. 2, ad 3; I, q. 78, a. 4.
[55]*Summa Theologica*, I-II, q. 72, a. 2, ad 4. As St. Thomas notes defective moral reasoning is due to passion: "He that has knowledge in a universal, is hindered, on account of passion, from reasoning about that universal, so as to draw the conclusion; but he reasons about another universal proposition suggested by the inclination of passion, and draws his conclusions accordingly. Hence the Philosopher says (Aristotle, *Ethics*, VII, 3, 1147a) that the syllogism of an incontinent man has four propositions, two particular and two universal, of which one is of the reason, e.g., no fornication is lawful, and the other, of passion, e.g., pleasure is to be pursued. Hence passion fetters the reason, and hinders it from arguing and concluding under the first proposition so that while the passion lasts, the reason concludes under the second."

Wherefore the understanding which is a part of prudence is a right estimate of some particular end.[56]

Prudential understanding or insight consists in a right estimate about matters of action. Like all knowledge it can be acquired in either of two ways; by discovering it oneself, or by receiving it from others.[57] St. Thomas finds that the two integral parts of *docility* and *sagacity* are necessary for the gathering of this prudential estimation or opinion.[58]

Docility. — While docility is useful in any learning, it is especially necessary for the acquisition of prudential insights.[59] The particular matters of action with which prudence is concerned are always contingent and singular and of an infinite variety. No man can consider them all sufficiently nor quickly enough for the total perfection of prudential action. Experience in these matters, which tends to limit the infinite possibilities of action to a finite number always takes time.[60]

Hence in matters of prudence man stands in very great need of being taught by others, especially by old folk who have acquired a sane understanding of the ends in practical matters.[61]

A disposition to learn from others more experienced in matters of action is a necessary condition for the acquisition of the virtue of prudence. This disposition to be taught, the will to accept the often undemonstrated and undemonstrable opinions of more learned and experienced men is the function of *docility* as an integral part of prudence. Though man has a natural aptitude for docility, constant effort in the form of frequent and reverent applications of the mind to the teachings of others is required to develop this disposition so necessary for the acquisition of prudence in human affairs.[62] No man, not even the learned can attain the perfection of prudence without docility, "since no man is altogether self-sufficient in matters of prudence."[63] Because of the uncertainty, the diversity and infinite

[56]*Ibid.*, II-II, q. 49, a. 2, ad 1.
[57]*Ibid.*, I, q. 117, a. 1.
[58]*Ibid.*, II-II, q. 48, a. 1.
[59]*Ibid.*, q. 49, a. 3, ad 4.
[60]*Ibid.*, q. 47, a. 3, ad 2.
[61]*Ibid.*, q. 49, a. 3.
[62]*Ibid.*, ad 2.
[63]*Ibid.*, ad 3.

variability of human activities no one can rely entirely on his own direction in the more trying and complex situations that confront him. The virtue of prudence cannot be developed without an active willingness to learn from the experience and knowledge of others.

Sagacity. — In the course of human activity it is often necessary to make a rapid conjecture about what is to be done in a particular situation. The time and opportunity for good counsel is limited by the exigency of the moment. To acquire a right estimate of what is to be done in such an instance man must depend upon himself alone. He must be disposed to make a right estimation in these circumstances. Ingenuity and sagacity of judgment are necessary to insure the rectitude of his estimation. Thus sagacity is also considered as an integral part of prudence.

> Now just as docility consists in a man being well disposed to acquire a right opinion from another man, so shrewdness is an apt disposition to acquire a right estimate by oneself. . . .[64]

To facilitate the intellectual acts of counsel and judgment leading to reasonable command of action the prudent man must be cognitively disposed by the virtues of good counsel (euboulia) and good judgment (synesis and gnome). As human habits these cognitive assistants of prudence are acquired through the voluntary repetition of acts. In the acts of good counsel and good judgment man must observe all the conditions necessary for their perfection.

To counsel and judge well about future actions man must *reason* well, proceeding from clear and pertinent knowledge of past experience provided by *memory,* the accurate *understanding* of the present validated by *docility* and personal *sagacity to* the certitude of judgment about the actions to be performed. Thus reason, understanding, docility, and sagacity function through the virtues of good counsel and good judgment as the cognitive elements of the virtue of prudence.[65] The resulting certitude about what should be done is applied by the virtue of prudence in the perfection of prudential command.

[64]*Ibid.,* II-II, q. 49, a. 4.
[65]Cajetan, *Commentarium in Summa Theologicam,* II-II, q. 128, no. 9.

Integral parts of Prudence as Commanding. — It is in the act of command, perfected by the virtue of prudence that the practical intellect and the will are most intimately cooperative for the production of human action. The intellect cannot apply the things counseled and judged to action without the motive power of the will.[66] Command is essentially an act of the reason, presupposing an act of the will.[67] It has been defined as an act directing "someone to do something by a certain motion of intimation."[68]

There are three things that concur for the command of reason in relation to actions. There is the order or direction of what is to be done, the intimation or declaration of this order, and the impulse or motion. The order and the declaration of this order belong to reason, while the motion comes from the will[69] through its preceding act of choice.[70] The will then proceeds through active use to move the other powers to the execution of the command of reason.

> After counsel's decision, which is reason's judgment, the will chooses; and after choice, the reason commands that power which has to do with what was chosen; and then, last of all, someone's will begins to use, by executing the command of reason; sometimes it is another's will, when one commands another; sometimes the will of the one that commands, when he commands himself to do something.[71]

The intimation or direction of what is to be done in a particular situation can be made by the reason in two ways. In one way the reason functions in the order of final causality, merely proposing or advising what should be done in this situation. In the other way the reason operates as an efficient cause, effectively and/or morally moving to the execution of action.[72] St. Thomas notes the twofold action of reason in this manner:

> Now reason can intimate or declare something in two ways. First absolutely; and this intimation is expressed by a verb in the indicative mood, as when one person says to

[66] *Summa Theologica*, II-II, q. 47, a. 1, ad. 3.
[67] *Ibid.*, I-II, q. 17, a. 1.
[68] *Ibid.*, a. 2.
[69] Aquinas, *Q.D. De Veritate*, q. 22, a. 12, ad 4.
[70] Cajetan, *Commentarium in Summa Theologicam*, I-II, q. 17, a. 1.
[71] *Summa Theologica*, I-II, q. 17, a. 3, ad 1.
[72] *Ibid.*, II-II, q. 83, a. 1.

another: This is what you should do. Sometimes, however, the reason intimates something to a man by moving him thereto; and this intimation is expressed by a verb in the imperative mood: as when it is said to someone: Do this.[73]

Because the human will enjoys freedom of specification (to will this or that good) and freedom of exercise (to will or not will)[74] concerning all particular goods that can be apprehended in this life, the command of reason is effectively efficient as a physical cause of action only when it proceeds from one's own reason in virtue of a previous free act in the will. The motive power of free choice carries over and gives effective efficiency to reason's act of command. The reasonable commands of others and of the law itself, are efficient moral causes which move the free agent to action in the manner of a final cause by urging, discouraging, or counseling actions. Moral causes can always be disregarded by man with his freedom and as a consequence do not always result in reasonable actions. Moral causes become effectively efficient causes of action only when an agent freely permits or chooses to let them operate in this manner.[75]

The proper function of prudence is to direct the means chosen by the free will to the end or goal that the will desires. This right ordering of means is found in the command of reason perfected by the habit of prudence. To perform its function well the virtue needs the active assistance of three perceptive conditions, *foresight, circumspection,* and *caution.* As integral parts of prudence these three conditions pertain to the act of command as their end, and in distinctive ways each implies an intellectual vision or supervision over the means.

Foresight. — Of all the parts of prudence *foresight* is the most important, and to it all the other parts are subordinate.[76] The very name of prudence as applied to this practical virtue is gathered from foresight or providence as its chief part.[77] As the principal part of prudence, foresight gives formal unity to the other prudential requirements and functions as the integrat-

[73] *Ibid.,* I-II, q. 17, a. 1.
[74] *Ibid.,* q. 13, a. 6.
[75] *Ibid.,* II-II, q. 50, a. 2.
[76] *Ibid.,* I, q. 22, a. 1.
[77] *Ibid.,* II-II, q. 49, a. 6, ad 1.

ing element of the virtue. Prudence through its integral part of foresight "foresees the events of uncertainties."[78] Thus the prudent man is able to exercise a participated kind of providence over his future contingent actions and direct them to the end of human life.[79] The clear vision of foresight assists the virtue of prudence to prepare for the future now. It does this by inspecting the chosen means as they are related and ordered to the desired end or goal of human action.

Circumspection. — As human actions are always concrete and never abstract they are surrounded by many circumstances. Though possible circumstances surrounding human actions are infinite the actual number that affect a particular action are limited.[80] These limited circumstances always exercise an influence upon the morality of the action itself. It may happen that an action which is good and suitable to the end in itself will become evil and unsuitable to the end because of the circumstances that surround it.[81] As a consequence the virtue of prudence must not only exercise foresight in ordering the means to the end, but it must also keep in view the circumstances that surround the means. It is the function of *circumspection* as an integral part of prudence to perform this task. Circumspection attends to the suitability of the means with their circumstances and is thus distinct from foresight which attends only to the suitability of the means.

> Just as it belongs to foresight to look on that which is by nature suitable to an end, so it belongs to the circumspection to consider whether it be suitable to the end in view of the circumstances.[82]

Caution. — Having viewed all the circumstances connected with a particular act to be performed, another perfection is needed to assist prudence in avoiding the extrinsic evils found in pursuit of good. The very multiplicity and infinite variety of human activity lends itself to the intermingling of good and evil.[83] The virtue of prudence must take special care in ap-

[78]*Ibid.*, q. 47, a. 1.
[79]*Ibid.*, q. 49, a. 6.
[80]*Ibid.*, a. 7, ad 1.
[81]*Ibid.*, a. 7.
[82]*Ibid.*, ad 3.
[83]*Ibid.*, a. 8.

plying prudential judgments to desirable ends so that all foreseen evil consequences may be avoided. As an integral part of prudence *caution* performs this function. The purpose of caution is not to avoid evil actions but rather the extrinsic evils that may impede the fruition of good actions. By the exercise of caution the prudent man takes care to avoid the ordinary evils that are extrinsic to his good actions. If this is not altogether possible he can, through the exercise of caution, lessen their harmfulness.[84] By observing due caution man is better prepared to meet the sudden and unforeseen evils that occur so often in human affairs.

> Caution is required in moral matters, that we may be on our guard, not against acts of virtue, but against the hindrance of acts of virtue.[85]

The reasonable exercise of foresight, circumspection, and caution about that which is most formal in the virtue of prudence, the commanded actions that proceed from man's deliberate reason, brings the virtue to its ultimate natural perfection. Beyond this the reason of man cannot go. Natural prudence with all its integral parts actively coordinated with its commanded and elicited acts enables man to perform all human actions with confidence and assurance.

[84]*Ibid.*, II-II, q. 49, a. 8, ad 3.
[85]*Ibid.*, ad 1.

CHAPTER VI

PRUDENCE THROUGH COUNSELING

Prudential Framework for Counseling

In all the integral parts of prudence and in the relationship of the parts to prudential acts there is evident need for conscious and deliberate ordering of both parts and acts of the virtue of prudence if the particular actions of the individual are to benefit. This conscious and deliberate ordering is nothing but the control that an intellectual agent should and must exercise over all activity that is essentially human.

He who has an intellectual nature, who can determine relationships and in a limited way exercise providence over his future actions has the responsibility of developing his potentialities according to the pattern of human virtue. This is the dictate of natural reason. To do otherwise natural forces must somehow be frustrated and perverted, with the result that the inevitable natural tensions found in human nature are increased rather than lessened.

It is prudence as an acquired virtue that directs man to the natural perfection of his human nature and to the attainment of limited but real human happiness. The joy and ease which this habit brings to human living makes it imperative that man should consciously and voluntarily cultivate the perfection of prudence in his soul.

The only direct approach to the virtue of prudence in the natural order is the constant and voluntary repetition of prudential acts with the active cooperation of the integral parts of the virtue. If, under the direction of practical reason, the integral parts of this virtue, good reasoning, memory of past experience and accurate understanding of the present verified through docility and personal sagacity, are exercised with reasonable foresight, circumspection and caution in all human activity, the function of prudence in its acts of counsel, judgment and command will be perfected. The individual will be operating according to the demands of his nature and a limited but real human happiness will result. Tensions and resistance will be mitigated by control; confusion will yield to clarity; doubts will be replaced by certitude; delay, negligence and inconstancy will be resolved in effective, orderly activity.

It is apparent from the evidence that has been presented that prudence is a very personal perfection of man, to be acquired by persistent and diligent effort. No one can efficiently cause the natural virtue of prudence in the individual soul but the individual himself. As director of moral life guiding every human action to the goal of reason, giving actuality to the acquired moral virtues and disposing for the intellectual virtues, both of which are so necessary for the rectification of man in his quest for human happiness and the removal of the extrinsic impediments to the operation of grace, the human virtue of prudence cannot be imposed from without. Only the individual can determine the practical sufficiency of reasonable counsel, make the decision that is reasonable for him, and issue the effective command of orderly action within the sanctuary of his own soul. There, under his Creator, he alone can and should be master. By his own reasonable actions he must realize the perfection of those potentialities that God has given him for human maturity and virtuous living. Others may help; indeed, others must help, but the individual alone can accomplish. The virtue which meets so completely the needs of human nature requires personal effort, experience, and time to reach its perfection.

Prudence and the Counseling Process

One of the specialized experiences which is directly ordered to the perfection of man in the virtue of prudence is the process of counseling. The very name of the process has been taken from the first act of the practical reason which is perfected through prudence for the reasonable consideration and decision about the means to successful and happy living. In the process of counseling the assistance of others is focalized in a very specific way to meet the natural needs of an individual human nature as it advances, often by faltering and fearsome steps, to the human maturity that is directed, ordered, and actualized by the practical intellect with its natural perfection of prudence.

If the process of counseling is to fulfill its function in a reasonable way it must recognize and follow the demands of prudential activity. The intellectual, moral, and psychological conditions of prudence in its acts of counsel, judgment, and command should be respected, fostered, and developed throughout the execution of the process. The arrangement, order, and realization of the counseling environment should be so effected that the essential elements and necessary conditions of prudential activity are activated, catalyzed, facilitated, and strengthened in a positive way.

At all times the counselor must be aware of his own limitations as he assists the vital and principal efficiency of the client in this process of human development. The activity of the counselor can never be the principal cause of the client's growth in the virtue of prudence and human maturity. The counselor, however, does function as a necessary instrumental cause in this process. Counseling, like teaching and the practice of medicine, is always a cooperative art. The ultimate success of counseling depends not so much upon the activity of the counselor but upon the orderly, enlightened mental activity of the client, the principal efficient cause of all intellectual, moral, and psychological development in the natural order.

Prudence and Counseling Methods

In facilitating the vital forces of growth and development the counselor could do no better in the exercise of his art than imitate the natural operation of the human mind in its production of prudential activity. Reasoning is to be activated, hindsight stimulated, insight promoted, and foresight intensified for the perfection of the client's personal mental activity in the consideration, selection, and command of the means that are morally right for him in his present situation as he approaches a good moral end. The discursive search for the truth concerning what is good for man here and now necessitates the alignment of the present situation in accurate perspective with past vicarious or personal experience, the enlightened estimation of the present in view of the proximate moral principles that govern it, and a very practical vision of proposed actions in these circumstances as effective means actively and cautiously ordered to a moral goal.

The methods adopted by the counselor for the execution of his task should be those that are apt to facilitate the command of morally good actions by the client in view of the hindsight, insight, and foresight that he has or will make his own through the counseling process. Since no man is sufficiently clever to know all things, even concerning himself and his own actions, nor does his experience cover every possible circumstance in which he may find himself, in prudential counseling due allowance must be made for the client's exercise of docility to the knowledge and experience of others in pertinent matters of action, as well as for the sharpening of his own personal sagacity in determining what is right for him in his own peculiar and distinctive situation.

More specifically the right counseling methods to be used in a particular instance with a particular client are those that are apt to facilitate the orderly descent from the summit of his soul which is reason, to the foot of the prudential hill, which is action. Provision must be made for all the intervening steps through which an orderly descent is to be accomplished. Memory of the past, understanding of the present, sagacity in considering future outcomes, reasoning to compare significant elements of the past, present, and future, and docility to the knowledge and opinions of others are or should be found in duly ordered counseling. This order is to be promoted by the co-operative activity of the counselor and the client with adequate awareness, respect, and appreciation of the intellectual, moral, and psychological contingencies affecting the client as he is here and now.

Counseling Theory and Practice Evaluated

The prudential requirements for counseling are not violated by the general points of agreement between traditional and client-centered concepts of counseling that were noted in the third chapter of this study.

Prudential counseling has a strictly personal aspect, the activity of the practical intellect in search of the truth about matters of action ordered to the command of reasonable human activity, and a personal-social aspect. The latter occurs as the individual seeks help from others when he finds that he is not competent to solve his difficulties alone. This aspect of counseling necessitates active face-to-face communication of at least two individuals, with mutual concern for the client and his problems, difficulties, or maladjustments. It always implies a superiority of knowledge, experience, or skill in the counselor which makes him apt to be of help to the client in his need. Above all, prudential counseling aims to help the client obtain the optimum personal development that is naturally realized in the acquisition of the virtue of prudence, so that he can handle himself and his problems in a more mature and satisfying manner.

Beyond these general points of agreement the prudential requirements for counseling seem to be both respected and rejected in different degrees by traditional and client-centered counselors. This is made more manifest in the consideration of the various differences that have been previously pointed out.

The nature of counseling. — The traditional counselor's view that counseling is an educational process and the client-centered view that counseling is a therapeutic process are not of necessity mutually exclusive. The counselor in his relation to the client, like the teacher in relation to the student, functions as an efficient instrumental cause in the development of human potentialities for growth in truth and being, a practical process that is essentially educational in nature. Both counseling and teaching are cooperative arts, which depend upon the orderly operation of vital activities within the client or the student, which function with principal efficiency in their grasp and acceptance of truth. Both are designed to promote learning, or the modification of behavior through experience.

In the exercise of his art the teacher aims formally and directly toward the establishment of the intellectual habits of understanding, science (both speculative and practical), wisdom and the arts. The counselor applies his art more directly to promote the acquisition and development of the most practical intellectual virtue of prudence, the only kind of truth that has the perfection of virtue since it directs and orders the actualization of the moral virtues in the rectification of human appetites. To assist in the resolution and modification of students' emotions and emotionalized attitudes is accidental to the formal work of the teacher. The same function, in varying degrees is essential to the work of the counselor who deals with intellectually confused and emotionally disturbed clients seeking or needing help in the solution of their problems and difficulties.

While the traditional counselors maintain that the client's necessary learning experience, which is radicated in the acquisition, penetration, and acceptance of truth, can be promoted by both teaching and assisting the client's intrinsic powers of discovery by the presentation of new, unrecognized, or unaccepted aspects of truth without harm to the counseling relationship, the client-centered counselors hold that consistent dependence upon the client's powers of discovery alone is possible within the therapeutic relationship. The former or traditional view seems to be more in accord with prudential requirements which necessitate docility to the knowledge and opinions of others as well as personal sagacity in finding the very practical prudential truth about matters of action. The view of client-centered counselors seems to eliminate prudential docility from the counseling relationship altogether, as they rely completely upon the personal sagacity of the client and his unverified powers of discovery to assist him in the grasp of this truth. The latter position would be tenable if to learn prudential truth were nothing but to remember something that is already known, or if each human being were a law unto himself.

In the first instance it would be necessary to presuppose that the client possessed knowledge of everything that is necessary for prudent action, including accurate understanding of himself, his motives and his actions, as well as all-embracing experience. In such a case the counselor's facilitation of the client's memory, or the recall and recognition of pertinent truth already possessed and the facilitation of reason would be suficient to promote prudent consideration, decision, and command of action by the client. Thus the counselor's function would be merely to assist in removing the impediments which are preventing the client from recalling and considering what he already knows and retains in his memory. To hold such a position seems to be contrary to good reasoning and common experience.

It is reasonable to presume that the client possesses some truth (imperfect speculative and practical science and wisdom), along with the radical natural potentialities to a more extensive and penetrating grasp of the same or additional truth (the natural habits of understanding, synderesis, and the powers of reason), as well as some experience in matters of action retained in memory. It is certainly the function of the counselor to help the client recall (facilitation of memory) and consider (facilitation of reasoning) the experience that he has had, and the knowledge that he possesses. This is probably best accomplished by assisting the client to remove the emotional impediments that are preventing him from making adequate use of these factors.

To presume, however, that the client has sufficient knowledge and experience to solve reasonably his present difficulties, not only in a way that appears to be psychologically satisfactory to him as an individual, but in a way that conforms to the reasonable psychological and moral demands of his rational human nature is not valid unless at the same time the alternative mentioned above is also presumed, that is, that each individual is a law unto himself — a position that is based upon complete moral subjectivism and relativism. Another equally erroneous alternative would be to maintain that every individual is infallible in his interpretation and application of the natural moral law as it is found in the soul of each human being.

The only apparent escape from these alternatives is the arbitrary limitation of the nature of counseling as proposed by the client-centered school which presumptuously if not erroneously limits counseling to the removal of emotional impediments or the modification of emotional attitudes and the promotion of a species of personal reorientation that would eliminate the traditional concept of "re-education" from the process itself. Such an escape does not seem to be justifiable within the limits of good reasoning and the prudential requirements which should determine the elements of prudential counseling. The contingency, the infinite variety of particular matters of action with which prudence is concerned put every man in very great need of being taught by others. Thus it seems unwise to overlook or interpret loosely the need for prudential docility as an integral and active element of the counseling process. Complete dependence upon the client's personal sagacity and unverified powers of discovery seems to be inadequate for prudential counseling, because, while this confidence may facilitate client awareness of the necessity of docility or the will to be taught, it fails to take positive steps toward strengthening or activating this necessary condition of prudential activity.

The aims of counseling. — Although both the traditional and client-centered counselors seem to be in accord with the ultimate aim of prudential counseling, consisting in the promotion of the client's optimum personal development, notable differences in the standard of measurement have been made evident.

The traditional school tends, without complete unanimity or understanding, to favor an objective standard of social and moral values as the criterion of client development in counseling. The client-centered schools, with their limited concept of the counseling process, find the subjective psychological comfort of the client in relation to his reality to be a sufficiently valid standard for this development. The former view, rightly understood, appears to be more closely allied with the prudential standard. Prudential development is measured by intelligent conformity to universally valid moral principles dictated by the nature of man and the natural moral law. Standards that are less objective, certain, or natural than these are not likely to promote the optimum personal development which is realized in the acquisition of total prudence and all of the acquired moral virtues.

Any theory of counseling that is not actively and directly concerned with the promotion of objectively determined moral rectitude in the client cannot be an effective or efficient aid directly ordered to his optimum personal development. A system of counseling that sacrifices the objectivity of the natural moral law as the measure of man's reasonable conduct leading to happiness cannot be complete. Trust and hope, no matter how well grounded, that adjustment will result in deeply socialized values is an insufficient justification for the elimination of the objective moral standard as it functions within the prudential counseling process. Intimate penetration and discriminating awareness of universal moral principles as they apply to the situation facing the client are essential elements in any counseling process that pretends to assist the client in his attainment of optimum personal development. Any deficiency in this respect can only result in an inadequate and imperfect type of counseling, incapable of assisting man toward true integration or a realistic personal reorganization. Failure to accomplish either of these objectives makes any hope for responsible prudential maturity through counseling chimeric, and consequently the process must fall short of its true goal.

The proximate aim of prudential counseling is to stimulate the client's personal mental activity for the consideration, selection, and command of morally good actions in his approach to a good moral end.

This is not a simple operation to be realized by a simple process. Any attempt to formulate a simple concept of this proximate aim tends to be an oversimplification. It has been pointed out, in recognition of this difficulty, that the proximate aim of the prudential counselor as he enters the counseling relationship is directed toward activating, catalyzing, facilitating and strengthening the essential elements and necessary conditions of prudential activity within the client. The counselor's intention is to do what he can as an efficient instrumental cause to assist the client toward a prudential solution of his difficulties. To this end, and in this order, the counselor's concern is that the client's reasoning must be activated, his hindsight stimulated, his insight promoted, and his foresight intensified.

Among the traditional counselors cited, the views of Mathewson on the proximate aim are most clearly formulated and seem to be more closely allied with prudential requirements. His proposal that the counselor aim to stimulate the client's powers of learning, adjustability, development, and integration on the level of conscious apprehension and evaluative reasoning, seems more likely to promote the accomplishment of the prudential aim. In this same matter Jones is guilty of over-simplification, while Strang seems undecided and vague. Williamson, though conceding other aims, appears to be primarily interested in helping the client acquire understanding and skill in the use of the five steps of clinical counseling. In the latter respect Williamson seems to propose the attainment of a skill or an art as the goal of the process, rather than prudential virtue. If this be true the deficiency is evident. Self-mastery is not a product of art but of the virtue of prudence.

In the limited client-centered view the proximate aim of the counselor is to demonstrate understanding and acceptance of the client and thus help to free him for normal growth and development by assisting in the recognition and removal of impeding emotional obstacles. That this procedure may be good and useful as the initial phase of prudential counseling is readily accepted. Recognition of the importance of good reasoning in prudential activity and of the often acute influence of emotional factors upon this ability makes it imperative that the counselor should in every way possible help the client to free himself from disturbing emotional obstacles. Activating the client's reasoning power is of primary importance within the proximate aim of the prudential counselor. If the client's power of reasoning is corrupted by the distraction or opposition of emotional disturbances, or if it appears to be destroyed altogether by impeding emotions, it is most necessary that these inordinate emotions be resolved as the initial step in facilitating the prudential processes.

To assume or imply, as the client-centered counselors do, that there is only one way for counselors to assist in the resolution or control of impeding emotions and stimulate the other processes of integration and reorganization is unwarranted.

It is a matter of common experience that reason, short of complete destruction by violent emotion, can dissipate emotional disturbances by turning to other thoughts. Forbidding the counselor to make any positive contribution in this direction may be logical in view of the client-centered concept of counseling, but it is nonetheless unreasonable by prudential criteria.

The second implication that once the emotional impediments are removed the other necessary processes of personal reorganization and integration will follow as a spontaneous response to the counselor's concentrated effort to convey emphatic understanding and acceptance of the client's attitudes and feelings may also be logically concluded from their principles. It suffers, however, from all the weaknesses and deficiencies previously observed in these principles.

In addition there seems to be a real danger that the client-centered counselors, by their exclusive concern for emotional factors, tend to over-emphasize these factors and the influence they have upon human behavior. It is possible that this tendency to concentrate upon emotional phenomena, would result in the de-emphasis of the noumenal elements that play such a vital part in reasonable control, as it flows from the highest use of the practical intellect, which is to be perfected through counseling for this precise task by the virtue of prudence. The consequences would be startingly disastrous for prudential counseling. It is probable that nature itself, unless perverted by evil persuasions, vicious customs, or corrupt habits, would prevent grave catastrophe, but it is also probable that the prudential counselor should make a positive attempt to observe and rectify defective insights or judgments even at the risk of being directive or offering an apparent challenge to the psychological independence of the client.

The methods of counseling. — Definitive determination of specific methods of counseling is beyond the scope of this study. To maintain otherwise is to overlook, or over-reach the possiblities and limits of rational analysis and evaluation. The final effectiveness of particular techniques as they function in the attainment of counseling aims is largely a matter of experimentation. To be valid the latter must be made within the framework of established principles. The principles governing the methods of prudential counseling have been pointed out above.

It is clear that the methods adopted by the counselor for his task should be those that are apt to facilitate the command of morally good actions by the client in view of the hindsight, insight, and foresight that the client has or will make his own through the counseling process. As Mathewson has indicated it may be necessary to use several methods throughout the process.

As an efficient instrumental cause cooperating with the client in the counseling process it may be necessary for the prudential counselor to assist in the removal of emotional obstacles impeding the client's power of reason, to stimulate good reasoning by offering new interpretations of knowledge or insights already possessesd by the client, to communicate additional specific knowledge or experiential opinions when they appear to be useful, and give positive intellectual assistance to the evaluation and correlation of the many factors pertaining to the prudential activities of the client as he deals with the situation confronting him. The counselor's selection of apt methods in particular instances with particular clients will vary with the differences in the intellectual, moral, and psychological contingencies affecting the client as he is here and now.

From the prudential point of view it seems unwise rigidly to maintain that any single technique will be apt in all cases to facilitate the client's prudential consideration, decision, and command of good moral action in all situations. In human affairs all situations and all individuals are not exactly the same.

Many other suggestions about methods made by the traditional counselors seem to be reasonable and useful for prudential counseling. Among these the views of Mathewson, again, appear to be more clearly and consistently stated and maintained. Thus they are more easily evaluated in terms of prudential demands. Mathewson has recognized the limits of theoretical considerations of counseling methodology and carefully observes them. He permits broad variations in the use of professional techniques to be determined by the counselor within the specific counseling relationship. The judgment of the counselor, evidence of effectiveness, and the observed needs of the client are the important factors in this determination. With certain reservations and not without apparent inconsistencies Jones, Strang, and Williamson seem to concur in this opinion.

The eager insistence that Williamson places upon adequate technical diagnosis and the six steps of clinical counseling tends to over-emphasize the importance of these factors for the purposes of prudential counseling. His stress upon the collection and critical review of exhaustive data ordered to more valid, meaningful, and complete interpretations about the client implies overconfidence in the validity of available technical devices. There is also the possibility that his very professional methodology magnifies the inadequacies of the client, and overreaches the psychological limitations of the instrumental causality exercised by the counselor within the counseling relationship. Williamson at times appears to give the erroneous impression that counseling is a creative art depending very largely upon the accuracy and thoroughness of the counselor's activity rather than a cooperative art subject in efficiency to the orderly, enlightened mental activity of the client. This impression may be due to his manner of expression and not be a reflection of his real concept of counselor causality. Available evidence is insufficient for definitive judgment.

In contrast to Williamson the views of Mathewson are more wisely and moderately expressed, and consequently appear to be more acceptable for prudential counseling. In his proposals Mathewson seems to recognize the psychological limitations of counselor efficiency as well as his reasonable potentialities for helping the client reach maximum development through the counseling relationship.

As previously indicated the attitude and methodology of the client-centered counselors appear to be very useful and profitable for the initial phase of prudential counseling. The emphasis that they have placed upon the creation of a non-threatening counseling atmosphere seems to be ideal for prudential purposes. It tends to keep the counselor aware of the limitations of his instrumental causality and to clarify the principal efficiency of the client in the counseling process. The acceptance, warmth, responsiveness, permissiveness, and freedom from pressure that they recommend as the dominate psychological characteristic of the atmosphere seem to be admirably suited for the initiation of prudential processes. Their rejection of technical diagnosis and the gathering of exhaustive scientific data about the client as prejudicial to the first phase of the counseling process seems to be reasonable and acceptable according to prudential norms. In addition their insistence upon concentrated counselor effort to provide and convey deep understanding of the client as he sees himself and acceptance of the attitudes he expresses at the moment seems to be a necessary part of the counselor's contribution to any counseling relationship. The consistent implication of the client-centered counselors that this technique is the sole or even the major contribution of the counselor that is allowable within the counseling relationship appears to be unjustified by prudential criteria. The latter view places unreasonable limits upon counselor causality and very often, unreasonable or impossible burden upon the client.

The sincere and understanding counselor who desires to do all he can to help the client develop and grow in prudential virtue will not hesitate to make positive contributions to the re-education of the client from his own technical knowledge and experience. If he is enlightened he will recognize his limitations and consistently observe them. He will neither overestimate his own position as a necessary, efficient instrumental cause in the exercise of this cooperative art nor underestimate the principal efficiency of the client. He will respect the client's psychological integrity and do all in his power to preserve and strengthen it as he assists him in his approach to the human maturity that can and will, in the natural order, be obtained only by the exercise of prudential actions leading to the perfection of total prudence and all of the acquired moral virtues.

BIBLIOGRAPHY

Books

Adler, Mortimer J. *Art and Prudence.* New York: Longmans, Green & Company, 1937. Pp. ii-250.

Allen, Frederick H. *Psychotherapy with Children.* New York: W. W. Norton & Company, 1942. Pp. 250.

Allers, Rudolf. *Psychology of Character.* New York: Sheed & Ward, 1943. Pp. v-383.

Allers, Rudolf. *Character Education in Adolescence.* New York: Wagner, 1940. Pp. 188.

Arbuckle, Dugold S. *Teacher Counseling.* Cambridge: Addison-Wesley Press, 1950. Pp. v-178.

Aristotle, *The Basic Works.* Edited by Richard McKeon. New York: Random House, 1941. Pp. vii-1487.

Aquinas, St. Thomas. *Opera Omnia.* Vives edition. Paris: 1872-1880. 34 vols.

Aquinas, St. Thomas. *Summa Theologica.* Translated by the English Dominicans. New York: Benziger Brothers, 1947. 3 vols.

Aquinas, St. Thomas. *Commentarium in Decem Libros Ethicorum Aristotelis.* Pirotta edition. Turin: Marietta, 1934.

Bennet, Margaret E. *Manual for Teachers and Other Guidance Workers.* Pasadena: Board of Education, 1941. Pp. 125.

Bernard, R., O.P. *Somme Theologique: La Vertu.* Editions de la Revue des Jennes. Paris: Desclee et Cie, 1933. 2 vols.

Bingham, Walter, and Moore, Bruce V. *How to Interview.* 3d ed. revised. New York: Harper and Brothers, 1941. Pp. 263.

Brennan, Robert E. *Thomistic Psychology.* New York: The Macmillan Company, 1941. Pp. vi-401.

Brennan, Robert E. (ed.). *Essays in Thomism.* New York: Sheed & Ward, 1942. Pp. vi-450.

Brennan, Robert E. *The Image of His Maker.* Milwaukee: The Bruce Publishing Company, 1948. Pp. vii-338.

Cajetan, Thomas de Vio. *Commentarium in Summa Theologicam.* Leonine edition. Rome: 1888. Vols. IV-XII.

Curran, Charles A. *Personality Factors in Counseling.* New York: Grune & Stratton, 1945. Pp. vii-287.

Curran, Charles A. *Counseling in Catholic Life and Education.* New York: The Macmillan Company, 1952. Pp. vii-462.

Current Trends in Psycohlogy. Edited by Wayne Dennis. Pittsburgh: University of Pittsburgh Press, 1947. Pp. ii-285.

Darley, John G. *Testing and Counseling in High School Guidance Programs.* Chicago: Science Research Associates, 1943.

Darley, John G. *The Interviewee in Counseling.* Washington, D. C.: U. S. Department of Labor, 1946. Pp. i-25.
Farrell, Walter, O.P. *A Companion to the Summa.* New York: Sheed & Ward, 1941. 3 vols.
Garrett, Annette M. *Counseling Methods for Personal Workers.* New York: Family Welfare Association of America, 1945. Pp. 187.
Garrigou-Lagrange, Reginald, O.P. *The Three Ages of the Interior Life.* St. Louis: Herder, 1947. 3 vols.
Germane, Charles E., and Germane, Edith G. *Personnel Work in High School.* Chicago: Silver Burdett Company, 1941. Pp. v-599.
Glueck, B. (ed.). *Current Therapies of Personality Disorders.* New York: Grune & Stratton, 1946. Pp. v-296.
Gredt, Joseph, O.S.B. *Elementa Philosophiae Aristotelico-Thomistica.* Barcelona, Spain: Herder, 1946. 2 vols.
Guidance in Educational Institutions. Edited by G. M. Whipple. The Thirty-Seventh Yearbook for the Study of Education, Part I. Chicago: The University of Chicago Press, 1938. Pp. iii-313.
Harney, Karen. *Self Analysis.* New York: W. W. Norton & Company, 1942. Pp. v-256.
Handbook of Child Guidance. Edited by Ernest Harms. New York: Child Care Publications, 1947. Pp. 751.
John of St. Thomas. *Cursus Theologicus.* Vives edition. Paris: 1885. 4 vols.
John of St. Thomas. *Cursus Philosophicus Thomisticus.* Edited by B. Reiser. Turin: Marietti, 1930-37. 3 vols.
Jones, Arthur. *Principles of Guidance.* New York: McGraw-Hill Book Company, 1945 (revised). Pp. xxv-592.
Lecky, Prescott. *Self-consistency: a Theory of Personality.* New York: Island Press, 1945. Pp. iii-154.
Lumbreras, Peter, O.P. *De Vitiis et Peccatis.* Rome: Angelicum, 1935. Pp. ii-230.
Lumbreras, Peter, O.P. *De Habitibus et Virtutibus in Communi.* Rome: Angelicum, 1950. Pp. v-210.
Mathewson, Robert H. *Guidance Policy and Practice.* New York: Harper and Brothers, 1949. Pp. 291.
Menninger, William C. *Psychiatry, Its Evolution and Present Status.* Ithaca, N. Y.: Cornell University Press, 1948. Pp. ii-138.
Merkelbach, Benedictus H., O.P. *Summa Theologiae Moralis.* Paris: Desclee de Brouwer, 1935. 3 vols.
Moore, Dom Verner. *Cognitive Psychology.* New York: J. B. Lippincott Company, 1939. Pp. v-636.
Moore, Dom Verner. *The Driving Forces of Human Nature.* New York: Grune & Stratton, 1948. Pp. 485.
Moore, Dom Verner. *Personal Mental Hygiene.* New York: Grune & Stratton, 1949. Pp. v-331.

Noble, Henry D., O.P. *Somme Theologique: La Prudence.* Editions de la Revue des Jennes. Paris: Desclee et Cie, 1925. 3 vols.

Pennington, L. A., and Berg, I. A. *Introduction to Clinical Psychology.* New York: Roland Press, 1948. Pp. v-595.

Porter, E. H., Jr. *An Introduction to Therapeutic Counseling.* Boston: Houghton Mifflin Company, 1950. Pp. 250.

Prescott, Daniel H. *Emotion and the Educative Process.* Washington, D. C.: American Council on Education, 1938. Pp. vi-323.

Prummer, Dominic M., O.P. *Manuale Theologiae Moralis.* Friburg, Brisgovia: Herder, 1935. 3 vols.

Rogers, Carl R. *Counseling and Psychotherapy.* New York: Houghton Mifflin Company, 1942. Pp. v-450.

Rogers, Carl R. *Client-Centered Therapy.* New York: Houghton Mufflin Company, 1951. Pp. viii-560.

Rogers, Carl R. *Counseling with the Returned Servicemen.* New York: McGraw-Hill Book Company, 1946. Pp. v. 159.

Sertillange, Antonin, O.P. *The Intellectual Life.* Translated by Mary Ryan. Cork: The Mercier Press, 1948. Pp. 1-182.

Snyder, William U. (ed.). *Casebook of Nondirective Counseling.* New York: Houghton Mifflin Company, 1947. Pp. v-339.

Snygg, Donald, and Combs, Arthur W. *Individual Behavior.* New York: Harper and Brothers, 1949. Pp. v-368.

Strang, Ruth. *The Role of the Teacher in Personnel Work.* New York: Teachers College, Columbia University, 1935. Pp. xvi-332.

Strang, Ruth. *Behavior Background of Students in Colleges and Secondary Schools.* New York: Harper and Brothers, 1937. Pp. xiv-555.

Strang, Ruth. *Pupil Personnel and Guidance.* New York: The Macmillan Company, 1940. Pp. xiv-356.

Strang, Ruth. *Educational Guidance: Its Principles and Practice.* New York: The Macmillan Company, 1947. Pp. xi-268.

Strang, Ruth. *Counseling Technics in College and Secondary School.* New York: Harper and Brothers, 1949 (revised). Pp. v-302.

Strang, Ruth. *Group Activities in College and Secondary School.* New York: Harper and Brothers, 1946. Pp. vii-361.

Strecker, Edward A. *Basic Psychiatry.* New York: Random House, 1952. Pp. 473.

Taft, Jessie. *The Dynamics of Therapy in a Controlled Relationship.* New York: The Macmillan Company, 1933. Pp. ii-296.

Traxler, Arthur E. *Techniques of Guidance.* New York: Harper and Brothers, 1945. Pp. 394.

Utz, Fridalino. *De Connexione Virtutum Moralium inter se secundum doctrinam St. Thomas Aquinatis.* Vechta in Oldenburg: Albertus-Magnus Verlag der Dominikaner, 1937. Pp. 135.

Vann, Gerald, O.P. *Morals Makyth Man.* London: Longmans, Green & Company, 1938. Pp. 250.

Williamson, Edmund G., and Others. *Student Guidance Techniques: A Handbook for Counselors in High Schools and Colleges.* McGraw-Hill Book Company, 1938. Pp. 305.

Williamson, Edmund G. *How to Counsel Students.* New York: McGraw-Hill Book Company, 1939. Pp. vii-562.

Williamson, Edmund G. *Counseling Adolescents.* New York: McGraw-Hill Book Company, 1950. Pp. vii-548.

Williamson, Edmund G., and Darley, J. G. *Student Personnel Work.* New York: McGraw-Hill Book Company, 1937. Pp. xxiv-314.

Williamson, Edmund G., and Hahn, M.E. *Introduction to High School Counseling.* New York: McGraw-Hill Book Company, 1940. Pp. x-314.

Williamson, Edmund G. (ed.). *Trends in Student Personnel Work.* Minneapolis: University of Minnesota Press, 1949. Pp. v-417.

White, Victor, O.P. *Psychotherapy and Ethics.* London: The Newman Association, 1945. Pp. 13.

Articles

Allers, Rudolf. "Confessor and Alienist," *The Ecclesiastical Review*, XCIX (November, 1938), 401-413.

Allers, Rudolf. "Irresistible Impulses: A Question of Moral Psychology," *The Ecclesiastical Review*, C (March, 1939), 208-219.

Allers, Rudolf. "The Vis Cogitative and Evaluation," *New Scholasticism*, XV (July, 1941), 195-221.

Allers, Rudolf. "Intellectual Cognition of Particulars," *The Thomist*, III (1941), 95-163.

Allers, Rudolf. "The Cognitive Aspect of Emotions," *The Thomist*, IV (1942), 589-648.

Allers, Rudolf. "Functions, Factors, Faculties," *The Thomist*, VII (1944), 323-362.

Allers, Rudolf. "Guidance and Counseling," *The American Ecclesiastical Review*, CXIII (August, 1945), 117-130.

Anderson, Harold H. "Directive and Non-Directive Psychotherapy: The Role of the Therapist," *American Journal of Orthopsychiatry*, XVI (October, 1946), 608-614.

Andrews, Jean Stewart. "Directive Psychotherapy: I: Reassurance," *Journal of Clinical Psychology*, I (January, 1945), 52-66.

Berdie, Ralph F. "Psychological Processes in the Interview," *Journal of Social Psychology*, XVIII (August, 1943), 3-31.

Bond, Leo, O.P. "The Effect of Bodily Temperament on Psychical Characteristics," *The Thomist*, X (1947), 423-501.

Bourke, Vernon J. "The Role of Habitus in the Thomistic Metaphysics of Potency and Act," *Essays in Thomism*. Edited by R. E. Brennan, O.P. New York: Sheed & Ward, 1942. Pp. 101-110.

Blocksma, D. D., and Porter, E. H. "A Short-term Training Program in Client-Centered Counseling," *Journal of Consulting Psychology*, XI (March, 1947), 55-60.

Castiello, Jaime. "The Psychology of Habit in St. Thomas Aquinas," *Modern Schoolman*, XIV (November, 1936).

Combs, Arthur. "Follow-up of a Counseling Case Treated by the Non-Directive Method," *Journal of Clinical Psychology*, I (April, 1945), 147-151.

Combs, Arthur W. "Some Contributions of Non-Directive Methods to College Counseling," *Journal of Consulting Psychology*, IX (September, 1945), 218-223.

Combs, Arthur W. "Basic Aspects of Nondirective Therapy," *American Journal of Orthopsychiatry*, XVI (October, 1946), 589-607.

Cowen, E. L., and Combs, A. W. "Followup Study of 32 Cases Treated by Nondirective Psychotherapy," *Journal of Abnormal and Social Psychology*, XXXXV (1950), 232-258.

Dunn, Marion F. "The Psychology of Reasoning," *Studies in Psychology and Psychiatry*, I, n. 1, 141.

Fabro, Cornelia. "Knowledge and Perception in Aristoletic-Thomistic Psychology," *New Scholasticism*, XII (October, 1938), 337-365.

Garrigou-Lagrange, Reginald, O.P. "La Prudence dans l'organisme des vertus," *Revue Thomiste*, XXXI (1926), 411-426.

Gerhard, William A., "Instinctive Estimation of Practical Values," *The Thomist*, VIII (1945), 185-232.

Gerhard, William A. "The Intellectual Virtue of Prudence," *The Thomist*, VIII (1945), 413-456.

Gilby, Thomas, O.P. "Thought, Volition, and the Organism," *The Thomist*, II (January, 1940).

Gillet, Martin, O.P. "La definitions de l'habitude d'aprés Aristote," *Revue des Science Philosophiques et Theologiques*, I (1907), 94-110.

Gillet, Martin, O.P. "Les elements psychologiques du caractere morale," *Revue des Science Philosophiques et Theologiques*, I (1907), 217-230.

Gorce, M., O.P. "Le Judgement Pratique," *Revue des Sciences Philosophiques et Theologiques*, XVII (1928), 5-37.

Grabmann, Martin. "Scientific Cognition of Truth," *New Scholasticism*, XIII (January, 1939), 140-165.

Hahn, Milton E., and Kendall, William E. "Some Comments in Defense of 'Non-directive' Counseling," *Journal of Consulting Psychology*, XI (March, 1947), 74-81.

Johan, Roger. "Nature da Judgement," *Revue de Philosophie*, XXXI (1924), 465-489.

Lottin, D. O. "La connexion des vertus avant Saint Thomas," *Recherchés de Theologie Ancienne et Medievale*, II (1930).

Lumbreras, Peter, O.P. "Notes on the Connection of the Virtues," *The Thomist*, IX (1948), 218-240.

Mailloux, Noel, O.P. "The Problem of Perception," *The Thomist*, IV (April, 1942), 266-285.

Mathewson, Robert H. "The Role of the Counselor," *Harvard Education Review*, XVII (Winter, 1947), 10-27.

Meister, R. K., and Miller, H. E., "The Dynamics of Non-directive Psychotherapy," *Journal of Clinical Psychology*, II (1946), 59-67.

O'Neil, Charles J. "Prudence the Incommunicable Wisdom," *Essays in Thomism*. Edited by R. E. Brennan, O.P. New York: Sheed & Ward, 1942. Pp. 185-204.

Ramirez, J. M., O.P. "De Philosophia Morali Cristiana," *Divus Thomas*, XIV (July, 1936), 87-122.

Robinson, Francis P. "Are 'Nondirective' Techniques Sometimes too Directive?" *Journal of Clinical Psychology*, II (October, 1946), 368-371.

Rogers, Carl R. "The Development of Insight in a Counseling Relationship," *Journal of Consulting Psychology*, VIII (November, 1944), 331-341.

Rogers, Carl R. "Counseling," *Review of Educational Research*, XV (April, 1945), 155-63.

Rogers, Carl R. "Psychometric Tests and Client-centered Counseling," *Educational Psychological Measurements*, VI (Spring, 1946), 139-144.

Rogers, Carl R. "Recent Research in Nondirective Therapy and Its Implications," *American Journal of Orthopsychiatry*, XVI (October, 1949), 581-588.

Rogers, Carl R. "Significant Aspects of Client-Centered Therapy," *American Psychologist*, I (October, 1946), 415-422.

Rogers, Carl R. "Some Observations on the Organization of Personality," *American Psychologist*, II (1947), 358-368.

Rogers, Carl R. "Some Implications of Client-Centered Counseling for College Personnel Work," *Educational and Psychological Measurements*, VIII (1948), 540-549.

Seeman, Julius. "A Study of the Process of Nondirective Therapy," *Journal of Consulting Psychology*, XIII (1949), 157-168.

Sheerin, Francis L., S.J. "The Development of the Will: Is Virtue Teachable," *Proceedings of the Western Division American Philosophical Association*, (April, 1941), 63-73.

Slavin, Robert J., O.P. "The Essential Features of the Philosophy of Education of St. Thomas," *Essays in Thomism*. Edited by R. E. Brennan, O.P. New York: Sheed & Ward, 1942. Pp. 135-150.

Snyder, William U. "An Investigation of the Nature of Non-Directive Psychotherapy," *Journal of General Psychology*, XXXIII (October, 1945), 193-223.

Snyder, William U. "The Present Status of Psychotherapeutic Counseling," *Psychological Bulletin*, XLIV (July, 1947), 297-386.

Snyder, William U. "Client-Centered Therapy," *An Introduction to Clinical Psychology*. Edited by L. A. Pennington and I. A. Berg. New York: The Roland Press, 1948. Pp. 465-497.

Strang, Ruth. "Criteria of Progress in Counseling and Psychotherapy," *Journal of Clinical Psychology*, III (April, 1947), 180-183.

Sturtevant, Sarah M., and Hayes, Harriet. "The Use of the Interview in Advisory Work," *Teachers College Record*, XXVIII (February, 1927), 551-562.

Thorne, Frederic C. "A Critique of Non-directive Methods of Psychotherapy," *Journal of Abnormal and Social Psychology*, XXXIX (October, 1944), 459-470.

Thorne, Frederic C. "Directive Psychotherapy: IX. Personality Integration and Self-Regulation," *Journal of Clinical Psychology*, II (1946), 371-383.

Thorne, Frederic C. "Directive Psychotherapy: XI. Therapeutic Use of Conflict," *Journal of Clinical Psychology*, III (April, 1947), 168-179.

Thorne, Frederic C. "Directive Psychotherapy: XIV. Suggestion, Persuasion and Advice." *Journal of Clinical Psychology*, IV (1948), 70-81.

Thorne, Frederic C. "Directive Psychotherapy: XV. Pressure and Coercion." *Journal of Clinical Psychology*, IV (1948), 178-188.

Thorne, Frederic C. "Principles of Directive Counseling and Psychotherapy," *American Psychologist*, III (May, 1948), 160-165.

Thorne, Frederic C. and Others. "Symposium: Critical Evaluation of Non-directive Counseling and Psychotherapy," *Journal of Clinical Psychology*, IV (1948), 225-263.

Whitaker, C. A., Warkentin, J., and Johnson, J. A. "A Philosophical Basis for Brief Psychotherapy," *Psychiatric Quarterly*, XXIII (1949), 439-443.

Williamson, Edmund G. "The Clinical Method of Guidance," *Review of Educational Research*, IX (April, 1939), 214-217, 248-249.

Wrenn, Gilbert C. "Client-Centered Counseling," *Educational and Psychological Measurement*, VI (Winter, 1946), 439-444.

Wrenn, Gilbert C. "Technique of Guidance and Counseling: The Interview," *Review of Educational Research*, IX (April, 1939), 201-204, 242-243.

Wrenn, Gilbert C. "Counseling with Students," *Thirty-Seventh Yearbook National Society for the Study of Education*, I (1938), 119-143.